The Spiritual Mind

The Spiritual Mind

Includes 21 Spiritual Laws From The Pathwork Guide Lectures

A Guide for Mental Health
and Emotional Well-Being

KATHLEEN KILEY FISHER

Copyright © 2017, Wellness Insights, LLC

All rights reserved. No part of this publication may be reproduced, stored in a retrieval system, or transmitted in any form or by any means, electronic, mechanical, photocopying, recording, scanning or otherwise without the prior written permission of the author except for the inclusion of a review.

The Pathwork® is a trademark owned and registered by The Pathwork Foundation and shall not be used without the express written permission of The Pathwork Foundation. Pathwork quotes used throughout the text with permission from the Pathwork Foundation. www.pathwork.org.

Requests to the author for permission should be addressed to:

www.kathleenkileyfisher.com, e-mail: kathleenkileyfisher@gmail.com

ISBN: Paperback 978-1-64184-043-9
      Ebook   978-0-99650-645-8

THE SPIRITUAL MIND
2nd Edition

Created by:
Kathleen Kiley Fisher
Founder and President
Wellness Insights, LLC
Mind Body Spirit for Health
www.kathleenkileyfisher.com
kathleenkileyfisher@gmail.com

MEDICAL DISCLAIMER

The contents of this book are intended to provide useful information to the public. All materials are for informational purposes only and are not a substitute for medical diagnosis, advice or treatment for medical conditions. The author and publishers specifically disclaim all responsibility for any and all liability, loss, or risk, personal or otherwise, that are incurred as a consequence, directly or indirectly, by the use or application of any of the material in this publication.

PATHWORK.ORG

The topics, principles, and summaries of the spiritual laws in this book were derived and conceptualized from multiple Pathwork lectures.

About Eva and the origins of Pathwork

The Pathwork lectures were delivered in trance through the channel of Eva Broch Pierrakos from 1957 to 1979. Eva was born in 1915 in Vienna, the daughter of the well-known Austrian novelist Jakob Wasserman. Driven by a private curiosity and a desire for deeper understanding of her world, Eva began to develop the gift of accessing an inner voice, at first through automatic writing and later by speaking in a trance state. In time the inner voice took shape as the authoritative, insightful, and loving persona of the Pathwork® Guide. She pursued the development of her gift with great devotion and perseverance, learning to listen and follow her guidance. Eva considered her ability to give spiritual guidance and to help people in their self-development as her life task.

Eva came to the United States in 1939 and continued her work in New York, giving Guide sessions and an ongoing series of trance lectures. She was a beautiful, vibrantly alive woman with a keen intelligence who enjoyed life in all its aspects. She loved people and animals and enjoyed food, skiing, swimming, and dancing.

In 1971 she married psychiatrist John C. Pierrakos, one of the founders of Bioenergetics and later, Core Energetics. The energetic work became an essential part of the Pathwork and contributed to its expansion.

Eva Pierrakos died in 1979, leaving behind her the rich legacy of more than two hundred Guide lectures, two flourishing Pathwork centers, and thousands of students and followers of the teachings.

ACKNOWLEDGEMENTS

I am deeply grateful to the authors and experts who appeared as guests on my television show, 'The Dream Show' during the five years that it aired. Many thanks for sharing your profound spiritual and medical insights. I am also indebted to my teachers who have graciously and patiently offered their professional guidance throughout the years including Cythnia Schwarzburg, Jack Clark, Rosemary Baue, Jorge Juncos, Erena Bramos, Kimberly Cahill, Pamela Chubbuck, John Pierrokos, and Wendy Hubbard. You have made a significant impact on my life and your contributions will forever nourish and remain with me. A very special thanks to all of my past, present and future students who continue to be my greatest teachers. To my husband, good friends and family members who patiently stepped aside while I wrote only to fully embrace me whenever I came up for air. Many heartfelt thanks to each of you. And most of all, I want to thank my spiritual teachers for the divinely inspired content that you continued to deliver through me throughout the entirety of this book. Without your continual presence, this book never would have come to be.

CONTENTS

A Personal Note From the Author xiii
Introduction 1

Part One:
The Spiritual Mind

Spirituality and Its Effects on Wellness and Behavior 7
Something Greater Than Love 8
The Language of Consciousness, Energy, and Light 9
Blocks to Enlightenment 14
Self Esteem, Self-Image and Energy Flow 18

Part Two:
Spiritual Transformation
21 Spiritual Laws From The Pathwork Guide Lectures

Abundance 40
Acceptance 43
Balance 47
Brotherhood and Sisterhood 51
Commitment 56
Compatibility 60
Free Will 63
Happiness 66
Love 70
Magnetism 73
Mobility 77
Mutuality 80

Peace 83
Perfection. 86
Prayer 89
Presence. 94
Relaxation 97
Responsibility. 100
Surrender. 103
Truth. 106
Unity. 109

Part Three:
When Will I Begin To Feel My Spiritual Self?

The Slow and Steady Process of Spiritual Development 115
Prayer – Pathway to Your Spiritual Self 117
Am I Getting Anywhere?. 123

Part Four: The Spiritual Mind in Dreams

The Importance of Dreams 127
Acknowledging Your Spiritual Mind in Dreams 132
Dream Worksheets. 138

Part Five:
Case Studies and Additional Practices

Spiritual Growth and Meditation Practices 147

A PERSONAL NOTE FROM THE AUTHOR

When I was fifteen years old, I was walking to my friend's house and I heard a voice. It came from the woods. It was clear, and it was male in tone. It said, "You won't have children of your own. You will help thousands who are already here." I looked into the woods but didn't see anyone. I wasn't afraid because it wasn't frightening. It was just unusual. Something different from anything I had experienced before. I didn't hear anything else until the following year.

When I was sixteen years old, I received another message while I was riding my bicycle home one summer day. This communication was quite different from the voice I'd heard a year earlier because it was not conveyed in human language. Nor was there a male or female tone to it. It was a very clear, direct, non-emotional thought transmission. If this thought was translated into words, it would have said something like, "Your mother will not live much longer after her children are grown." The transmission of this 'thought form' was palpable as it traveled up through my spine and into my brain.

Just like the previous year, I didn't respond emotionally to this information. I admit that I was more curious about this thought transmission than the voice I'd heard from the woods. I suspect it had something to do with the threat of losing someone I had already loved and known for the past sixteen years of my short, beautiful life.

* * *

On the evening of December 25, 1978, I was in a serious car accident. It was snowing outside and my high school boyfriend was driving me home from a Christmas party. The snow of winter can fall generously in Connecticut, and this Christmas night was no exception. As we were driving on a main road in my hometown of Ansonia, my boyfriend turned the steering wheel of his sporty, new Sunbird to negotiate a bend. The steering wheel turned at the command of his hands, but the car did not. We smashed into a telephone pole. Unsecured in my seat (we didn't wear seat belts in 1978), I flew directly into and partially through the front windshield.

I don't remember anything immediately after the impact. When I woke up, there were people in white standing over me with tweezers in hand. They carefully removed splintered glass from my face, the majority of it coming from my forehead. When I asked, "What happened?" a nurse gently responded, "You were in a bad car accident. You may have broken your jaw." She then gestured *'Sshhh'* with an index finger and pointed to her own jaw, "Keep it still." I acquiesced by closing my eyes. *Ugh.*

I don't know how many of you have had your mouth wired shut, but it's impossible to eat and almost as impossible to drink. You have to slurp your meals, which are nothing more than pureed liquids, or in my case Gerber baby food, into the tiny little spaces between your teeth. A strong, projected overbite certainly would have come in handy.

It's also wise to stay close to home if your mouth is wired shut. I always kept a pair of pliers nearby just in case I had to vomit. The thought of prying my wires open was horrifying, but not nearly as terrifying as cutting them out in public. Hearing a voice speak to me from the woods? No big deal. Feeling a thought form penetrate my central nervous system? Ok.

Having to cut wires fast enough so I didn't choke to death? Scary. Cutting them out in a public place? Even worse.

Besides, I was too weak to go anywhere.

Did I mention you can't talk with a wired jaw? If you try, you end up sounding like one of those victims on an NCIS episode who's bound and gagged in a closet and can't scream for help. Talking is only an option if you prefer to mumble and I didn't. So after the first week of my mouth temporarily out of service, I stopped trying. I surrendered, accepted, and finally relaxed into a state of silence which I soon learned had many sounds of its own.

My fifteen- and sixteen-year-old experiences became clearer. Transmissions come from within.

It was during the next five weeks at the ripe young age of seventeen that I became acutely aware of the benefits of silence. Sounds of the unseen are unlike the sounds in outer life. Inner sounds aren't so silent when you really begin to pay attention. And that I did. I observed the interactions between my family members – my mother, two brothers, and sister, along with my friends and theirs, and whoever else came by to visit during those next five weeks. I realized quickly that the reality of inner life communication wasn't that much different from outer life, except *ignorance has many people believing they can actually cover up their thoughts and feelings.*

In my silence, I had the opportunity to observe, sense, feel, and hear how others authentically communicated with each other while I sat and slowly recuperated on the living room couch. People really do communicate what they mean. We are just not self-aware enough nor fully cognizant yet to weed out and only respond with laser beam focus to the most genuine and truthful thoughts that maintain loving, long-term relationships.

I realized during this short, five week span of time that although I couldn't talk and initially considered myself disengaged, I really wasn't at all. Being aware, acknowledging or noticing others is as engaging and active as having a dialogue with them. I wasn't excluded from any conversation in the room, *unless I thought I was*. I learned that it's actually impossible to be left out when you are acknowledging another, *even if he or she is not acknowledging you*. The intention to acknowledge another person automatically makes the connection. There is no such thing as 'passive observation' because awareness of others automatically introduces you to their thought fields. I was actively participating with the others in the room. Their thought forms were eliciting responses from me. Silent, mouth-wired-shut responses, but very real, direct, and highly engaged responses.

I didn't know at the time that some people referred to these experiences as spiritual. I just knew that I liked this part of myself. I found a deep place of calm that I could go to 'within'. It was familiarly comfortable without my knowing why, like the adopted child who immediately senses her biological mother when reintroduced to her; the subtle soft frequencies of the warm hollow cavity from whence she came triggers memories of the womb of which she was once a part —where nurture and nature molded her physical life — that which simply cannot be erased by any matter of separation.

When the six weeks were up, I went to my surgeon's office to have the wires removed. Afterwards I sat up in the chair and slowly opened and closed my jaw a few times. I happily stood up, thanked the surgeon, and fainted.

* * *

Years later during my meditation sittings, I would always feel sensations in the center of my forehead between the brows, also known as the 'third eye'. I felt quite a pinch one day, so I got up to look at my face in the mirror. There, sticking out of my forehead was a thick, jagged piece of glass. The windshield that was instrumental in introducing me to my spiritual self when I was seventeen years old had reappeared, but this time from the inside out. I tried removing the shard of glass from my forehead, but it wouldn't budge. Even though a good portion was visible, the glass was lodged so deeply within my head that I had to go to the Emory Clinic in downtown Atlanta to have a surgeon remove it. This piece of glass had remained embedded in my head for almost twenty-one years. So for anyone who's wondering whether meditation opens the third eye or not, it does. I have the glass to prove it.

There are many other stories that pertain to my spiritual experiences and growth, but I only want to write about things that will help you in yours. The example of my mouth being wired shut for six weeks was a life experience that took me into the depths of myself. We all have experiences that bring us as close, or even closer to the spiritual existence living within. These experiences should be recognized and acknowledged. And that's what this book is about.

It's my hope that you will find the words, understanding, acceptance, and wisdom to help you integrate the best and boldest part of yourself into your daily life, both personally and professionally.

* * *

The case studies and examples included herein are taken from individual sessions. The name of each client has been changed for confidentiality purposes. Some of the examples have been slightly altered to further protect the client's anonymity. Each example demonstrates an issue or multiple issues and the behavioral changes that were made as a result of restoring spiritual principles in areas that lacked awareness.

INTRODUCTION

In the pages that follow, you will find a systematic approach to access your spiritual self. Many practical, self-soothing exercises are included to connect you with your divine intelligence. This self-discovery process is meant to help you achieve inner balance, peace and calm. While in this relaxed state, you can access the innate wisdom of your mind and body to heal and liberate deep-seated soul issues.

Spirituality is a vast topic and can lend itself to various interpretations. To avoid any confusion, I've provided explanations for most of the terminology used herein. This book is not meant to take you away from your current spiritual or religious practice. If you already belong to a faith-based organization, continue with your affiliation if it supports your spiritual growth. This book is also not meant to be a substitute for prescription medications although the exercises can certainly be used to access inner peace. I know because I've applied these techniques for the past twenty-two years as an alternative to prescription drugs. For me, prescription drugs were never an option because I've lost too many family members to drug addiction. Instead, I chose prayer. Prayer, and the many other mind body techniques included throughout this book.

Personalized Prayer

Prayer may mean something entirely different to you, but mine is deeply personal and so are the prayers and meditations offered herein. They are specifically meant to help you realign with your center. Each prayer is designed to help you identify and dissolve anxious or depressive thoughts while you maintain a connection with your inner divinity.

I know that the word prayer can often be likened to that of a one-way street. It's hard to believe in something that you can't visually see or physically touch. I'm reminded of the late legendary ABC news anchor Peter Jennings who once said (I'm paraphrasing here), "I have no idea how it is that I sit in a building in New York City and end up in your living room every night." Yet no one seems to really care. People watch anyway. Well believe it or not, prayers are transmitted quite similarly. The transmission of prayers can be likened to that of a television set minus the hardware.

You will see throughout the contents of this book that prayer is not used as a 'stop & drop' your latest worry. Nor is it something you routinely recite only on Saturdays and Sundays. Prayer in this context is practiced to develop a relationship with your spiritual self – so that your wisdom and creativity become part of your daily life. So that the last word 'spirit' in the term mind-body-spirit is as real to you as the words 'mind' and 'body' are.

When used as a wellness tool, prayer becomes a very useful mind-body technique that unites you with your spirit. As you experience the reality of your spiritual self, you become more confident that your divinity is as accessible and alive as any other part of you.

Also included in this text are twenty-one of the eternal, universal spiritual laws. For the purposes of our work together, the word 'law' herein refers to a lasting principle that is permanent and unchangeable, rather than a rule that a criminal might break. Law in this sense refers to immutable truth; the sturdy footing upon which your inner foundation solidly stands, regardless of where your outer self may be at any given moment.

Practical exercises are provided with the spiritual laws to help you integrate each eternal truth into your daily thoughts and feelings. The spiritual laws and exercises are meant to be reviewed and practiced again and again until you know them by heart. Developing the habit of self-introspection will help you access your inner wisdom. Whenever you are feeling disharmony within, you will know which questions to ask yourself to regain balance, confidence, and calm.

Please take your time while doing each exercise. Applying spiritual law to your everyday life requires time, practice, and a lot of self-honesty. Reflect, consider and 'feel into' your responses. Allow yourself to be open-minded and wide-hearted. Don't rush through this all-important process.

While practicing the 'Thoughts to Think' exercises, state each one with meaningful intention. Feel free to speak the words aloud. You deserve the necessary time to consider your personal beliefs about God, your soul, and your divine expression in your daily interactions with others. It's important to know your spiritual self and how it contributes to your overall health and well-being.

Your spiritual development process can be practiced on your own, in a group setting, and in professional one-on-one sessions. You may choose to discuss your spiritual development with a trusted friend or spouse who supports such inner exploration. If you choose to do most of the work on your own, please see a trusted professional if and when you feel 'stuck'. Discussion and self-awareness will help you eliminate what's not real and support what is. Sharing your true self with a trusted confidant can be most beneficial in the spiritual growth process. A humble attitude and courageous spirit will open the inner door. You just have to be willing to walk through it.

PART ONE
THE SPIRITUAL MIND

"After you have reached a certain stage on your path of development, you discover within yourself a power and intelligence other than your usual conscious mind which feels as though it were a separate being."

The Pathwork Guide, Balance of Inner and Outer Control

SPIRITUALITY AND ITS EFFECTS ON WELLNESS AND BEHAVIOR

Spirituality is a living reality that is full of feelings, aliveness, and a deep sense of interconnectedness. Spiritual qualities such as love, vitality, compassion, and kindness already exist deeply within you. Whenever you have difficulty accessing any of these positive traits, it is due to ignorance *or a violation* of one or more of the spiritual laws. The word 'law' in the universal sense does not mean 'something to obey'. Law in the spiritual sense is a principle, something that is unchangeable, immutable. It simply is.

In the pages that follow, you will learn how to identify misconceptions that separate you from your divine intelligence. Practical exercises are provided after each section to help you understand *why* you act and behave in certain ways. You will become aware of the root causes that block the wisdom of your spiritual mind. Dissolving your misconceptions will prepare you to experience high voltage spiritual energy while still living in the physical body. As you integrate the attributes of your spiritual self, you'll increasingly expand your capacity to love, create, and express your true self. You'll come to know through personal experience that the eternal life force is *an internal source* that is always readily available to you.

SOMETHING GREATER THAN LOVE

Love is the highest and most expansive emotion a human being can experience, but it is not the highest state of consciousness one can attain. In the spiritual world, where everything is unified and experienced as a complete whole, love is so much more than a feeling. On this higher plane of reality, love is the binding agent that glues all of the other senses together. Touch, sight, scent, sound and feeling are experienced as one complete whole. They are not separate like we experience them in the physical body. As this truth is sought deep within yourself, you approach the unified state of consciousness.

The unified plane is the world of the divine center, the larger self. When the connection to your spiritual mind is strong, you sense it. You can intuit this part of yourself. As your self-awareness increases and your emotions mature, divine intelligence becomes much more accessible. This sacred integration occurs to the degree you're willing to let go of your preconceived ideas.

The unified state is difficult to explain because it's a mind-body-spirit experience all at once, all at the same time. Our conscious mind alone is too narrow to experience it and our vocabulary is too limited to describe it. In fact, words are not even necessary in the oneness state because everything is experientially understood. There's no need for explanation.

THE LANGUAGE OF CONSCIOUSNESS, ENERGY, AND LIGHT

In the nonphysical world, spiritual language is a picture language. Consciousness and energy are expressed through images and symbols, or 'thought-forms'. The energy of each thought molds itself into the form that it represents. For instance, aesthetic images illuminated by brilliant colors of light represent eternal truths. They are not only stunning in appearance, they are multi-sensorial. They emanate harmonious rhythms and sounds. They emit the purest scents. Fluid and agile, they are capable of manifesting into any shape of their choosing through the malleable life substance that sustains them.

Thoughts that lack in the energy of truth and love are much less vibrant. Such forms vary in density and translucency, and are outlined in dull, dark greyish tones that accentuate the degree of the distortion they represent.

Most of us are familiar with the language of the non-physical world through dreams and meditations. Meditators have frequently reported 'seeing' images, both human and other-worldly figures while sitting in stillness. Meditators also witness 'the kaleidoscope effect' where swirling colors pass through the mind's eye during meditation. Dreams also provide messages through symbols and figures. These familiar and not-so-familiar images have been relied upon for centuries to deliver personal messages from the unconscious. Guidance, advice and helpful hints that have been specifically beneficial to the dreamer.

Communication from the non-physical world may seem vague and even nonsensical at times, but only because it's not understood. As you work through feelings of discomfort while learning your 'inner speak', personal imagery becomes much easier to understand. To find more information on how to interpret your dreams, you can go to: *Part Four: The Spiritual Mind in Dreams*.

Words Are Important

Words are the clothes that you wrap around your ideas. They represent your inner self. The style and tone you choose will impress upon others who you are and where you stand. Words you choose to lift, inspire, support, and encourage resonate with your deepest truth. When such sentences are spoken, the energy that transports your words is powerful, clear, clean and pure. Authenticity resonates through you, nurturing your entire body while elevating your relationships to a higher plane.

Words that are spoken insincerely, with deception or negative intention contain very low energy. They are transported by weak frequency bands. They may sound 'right', but you don't *feel* good when you hear them. You have a 'gut' feeling that something is off. Your wisdom 'reads' the weak energy of the intention and senses a 'cover-up', while your conscious mind receives the masked, phony word. Inner truth perceives inconsistency. You intuit that the incoming signal doesn't match the meaning of the word.

Frequency and Tone

Your words are powerful thoughts full of strong energy that continually produce outcomes – impactful outcomes that matter. Every word spoken represents a thought, its intention, and the electro-magnetic frequency that delivers it. When your spiritual self detects a phony incoming message, your emotional body may not be clear enough to register it. Distortions and misconceptions create foggy inner terrain that blocks the truth from flowing freely. Emotional immaturity can't sense the impure actions and motives of others, but it's still noted by your spiritual mind. The more you clear your own distortions, the easier it becomes to read the impurities of others. Words associated with peace, enlightenment, and love start to 'feel lighter' than words associated with negativity, shame and deceit. Energy fields are keenly sensed and become just as real as all other physical attributes. Your energy body, the carrier that transports the frequency and tone of your thoughts and words, no longer remains anonymous.

Peace Does Not Mean Boring

The choice of words and phrases you use are very much connected to your environment, upbringing, and culture. Whether positive or negative, your personal association with words will cause you to respond in very specific, *subjective* ways. For example:

During a private session, my client was experiencing anxiety and angst due to a break-up with her long-time beau. I offered an exercise that would decrease her anxiety and increase a steady flow of peace. She immediately declined. When I asked why, she replied, "Because peace is boring. I will feel dead inside." The state of peace is often misunderstood. I've had other clients respond similarly. One client compared being peaceful to that of his grandparents. "I'm only 54 years old. I don't want to be acting like my grandparents. Not yet anyway." I should mention that both of these people are highly educated professionals.

It's more common for clients to tell me what they *don't* want when I ask them what they're looking for: "I don't want to feel anxious anymore", "I don't want to be arguing all the time", or "I don't want to feel so confused when trying to make a decision". It's a rare occasion to hear a client say they want inner peace – the state of being where the spiritual self is most present.

The Boundaries of Language

Every profession has a terminology of its own. Law, medicine, finance and many other vocations use industry-specific language. To become involved in any of these fields, you have to learn its vocabulary. Imagine setting a goal to work out and lose twenty pounds without understanding the terminology of a fitness instructor. "Shake that booty, curl those abs, make those buns hard as steel." Seriously?

In order to interact or successfully engage with people, it's necessary to understand the language they speak. Learning the lingo is important, especially when it comes to spirituality and religion. Words that are used to describe deeply held personal beliefs such as an almighty creator or how existence began and/or may end are usually charged with passion, conviction and emotion and will often cause inner unrest.

Words will never fully convey the entire meaning or experience of the spiritual self, God, or any other cosmic truth. One word cannot possibly convey all. This does not mean that you shouldn't have a spiritual vocabulary to rely upon. Words are necessary if you want to grow and develop spiritually. Each word used constructively to build the bridge to your spiritual mind is a word well-spoken.

Spiritual Vocabulary

Test Yourself! The list below contains references commonly used in religious and spiritual practices throughout the world. Write down the meaning of each word or phrase that you are familiar with in the blank space provided. Take your time. You can revisit the list and add more definitions as you expand your spiritual vocabulary.

Acceptance _____

Allah _____

Authentic _____

Awareness _____

Bliss _____

Blocked _____

Breath _____

Buddha _____

Christ _____

Compassion _____

Consciousness _____

Cosmic _____

Creator _____

Dark Force _____

Defensive _____

Denial _____

Devil _____

Divine _____

Doubt _____

Ego _____

Eye for an eye _____

Fear _____

Feminine _____

Free Will _____

God _____

Helpless _____

Higher Power _____

Image _____

Imagination _____

Law _____

Light _____

Love _____

Magnetism _____

Maker _____

Meditation _____

Mindfulness _____

Peace _____

Self-esteem _____

Self-image _____

Spirit _____

BLOCKS TO ENLIGHTENMENT

The most common misconceptions about the word 'God', or a higher spiritual power in general often arise in early childhood. The dynamics and interactions that occur within a family unit usually leave deep and lasting impressions about whom or what 'Spirit' or 'God' is. Through the eyes of a child, both parents and God are authoritarians and are often misinterpreted as being alike. The immature mind of a child will conclude that if a parent is wise, giving and loving, then God must be too. If a parent is frugal, absent, or cruel, then so must be God. These deeply imbedded, personal beliefs develop and coincide even when a child receives traditional religious dogma that claims God is separate and apart from the whole of humanity.

Children rarely recognize that their parents have some growing up of their own to do. It would be uncommon to find a child who is mature enough to recognize that her parents are not yet completely evolved. And even when this fact is realized as an adult, the child consciousness buried within may still not agree. Internal conflict about what God is will remain until childhood misconceptions are brought to the surface, reassessed by the mature mind, and re-educated with the truth.

Deeply ingrained 'God' images such as a 'stern dictator', 'too busy with others', 'absent' or 'unavailable' will often interfere with your efforts in trying to develop a deep spiritual connection. There are many personal beliefs and experiences from childhood that remain buried within the unconscious of the adult mind. The exercises on the following pages will assist you in bringing your childhood spiritual beliefs to light. Comparing your current beliefs to those of your parents or other caregivers can be a valuable tool in understanding your perception of 'God'.

In the chart below, fill in as much information as you can remember about the day-to-day lifestyles of your primary caregivers and their spiritual or religious practices.

YOUR PRIMARY CAREGIVER'S DAY-TO-DAY STYLE

	Primary Caregiver's Religious and/or Spiritual Beliefs and Practices	Primary Caregiver's Style in Day-to-Day Living: (Examples: Absent, Cruel, Fair, Helpful, Kind, Manipulative, Positive, Relaxed, Stern, Strict)
Parents: 　Mom 　Dad		
Other Primary Caregivers: **Foster Care Parents** **Adoptive Parent(s)** **Grandparents:** 　Grandmother 　Grandfather		
Close Relatives: 　**Siblings** 　**Aunts, Uncles**		
School Teachers:		
Other:		

In the chart below, complete both columns with as much information as you can recall. In the first column, list your current beliefs for each category. Then complete the second column (how you remember it). Once you have completed both columns, compare the similarities and differences. Then continue on to the next page and answer the questions.

BELIEFS, BEHAVIORS AND HABITS

	List Your *Current* Religious or Spiritual Beliefs that Influence your Decision Making About:	List Your Primary Caregiver's Attitudes, Beliefs, and Behaviors About (During the Time They Cared For You):
Money		
Sex		
Church Participation **Other Spiritual Participation**		
Prayer **Meditation**		
Social Etiquette and Behavior		

Once you've completed the BELIEFS, BEHAVIORS, AND HABITS chart, answer the following questions.

EXERCISE

1. Is your current spiritual or religious practice similar to your experience as a child and teenager?

2. Do your religious/spiritual practices support you in developing a close, personal relationship with God and your spiritual self?

3. Review your mother, father and/or caregiver's parenting styles and religious/spiritual practices. Then write down your beliefs about how you think 'God' treats you; is or isn't there for you; and what H/She expects from you.

   Do you notice any similarities between the styles and practices of your parents/caregivers and how you perceive God to be? If so, write them down.

4. How fulfilling is your current spiritual or religious practice?

5. Do you feel you have a close and personal relationship with your higher power or do you feel like it's something foreign and 'out there'?

6. What makes your spiritual practice real and personal?

SELF ESTEEM, SELF-IMAGE AND ENERGY FLOW

Child Consciousness

The mind makes observations and conclusions at *all* ages. Conclusions made during childhood and adolescence are formed by the level of awareness that is perceiving at that time. Without the maturity to objectively consider other viewpoints, many beliefs are shaped by incomplete and unverified information.

The following is a very basic and seemingly harmless conclusion made by five-year-old Johnny:

Johnny is playing on the swings, enjoying the sun on his face, loving the warm breeze that brushes his little body as he sways through the air. Johnny pumps his feet back and forth, embracing the joy that such freedom brings, until Johnny's mother appears. She has come to take Johnny to his cousin's birthday party where there will be clowns, balloons, games, cake and ice cream. Johnny is too young to make the connection that he is leaving one fun experience for another. All he knows is that the exhilaration he is experiencing is coming to an end. Johnny kicks and screams and cries. He thrusts his arms at his mother in an attempt to maintain his current state of pleasure. His mother sternly reprimands him. Johnny learns that it's wrong to hit mommy, and subconsciously perceives: It's wrong to fight for pleasure.

Distortions formed during childhood and adolescence often remain buried within the subconscious. These misconceptions often contribute to low self-esteem and unworthiness.

Self-Esteem

There is a notable distinction between self-esteem and a self-image. The main difference is that self-esteem is a feeling experience. When your authentic feelings are expressed instead of suppressed, they are allowed to grow, transform, and mature.

Healthy self-esteem is nurtured by self-acceptance. The willingness to accept and feel *all your feelings* creates an inner opening that allows your deep, true self to emerge. Your mind and your body remain open and clear as you develop resilience and build self-confidence.

Low self-esteem develops when unpleasant feelings are ignored and remain buried and 'stuck'. Blocks in the human energy field build up and life force can't flow. While such uncomfortable feelings fester, negative thoughts continue to breed, creating friction and distressing situations.

Emotional Reactions versus Genuine Feelings

Emotional reactions are often misinterpreted as genuine feelings. Although emotional reactions feel real, they are defense mechanisms you created to avoid experiencing a deeper part of yourself. Your real feelings may not feel pleasant at times, but releasing them is necessary to remain connected to the core of your real being.

An emotional reaction may feel genuine and it can hurt when someone doesn't respond the way you expect. But this 'someone' is not responding to who you really are. Any effort you spend trying to promote who you're not is precious time taken away from your true self.

Feelings create your reality. If unresolved issues, pain, or sadness from the past are not dealt with, you will continue to create very similar experiences in your future.

Below is a list of common emotional reactions that are often mistaken as genuine feelings:

Aggression	Exaggeration	Overwhelm
Angry outbursts	Domination	Submission
Blame	Hostility	Tension
Criticism	Irritability	Urgency
Cruelty	Obsession	Withdrawal

Learn what your emotional reactions are so you can begin to dissolve them. Name an emotional reaction every time it shows up, *"I'm frustrated - I'm having an emotional reaction."* Or, *"I'm overwhelmed – I'm having an emotional reaction"* and so on. The more you call out each reaction for what it is, the sooner you can detach from your defensive postures.

Pray and ask your higher self to guide you to the truth within yourself. You can also practice the exercises at the end of this section, *'Dissolving Images and Energy Blocks Through A Daily Record'*. The exercises will help you align with your authentic feelings.

Identifying your emotional reactions is necessary for spiritual growth. We will discuss how you can do this on the following pages, but first let's take a look at why they exist.

Self-Image

Self-images are created from an idea, concept, or mental picture of yourself. Since early childhood, you've learned to think of yourself in concrete, definitive ways. You've created a mental scrapbook of self-images that represent who you think you *should* be. Since you believe these images about yourself, you expect others to 'see' you in the same way.

Self-images greatly influence the choices you make in your life including what you're willing to feel and what you will not. For example, a man may believe he is worthless because his father abandoned his family when he was a child. This deeply ingrained misconception can cause him to inaccurately assess his work performance. Even though he may receive positive reviews from his boss, he will reject it. As long as he identifies with his 'unworthy' self-image, he'll have difficulty accepting anything other than the identity he has created of himself. In fact, he may even feel threatened if someone tries to change it because it's the only identity he knows. If his boss gave him a raise, it could make him feel worse because that would contradict what he thinks about himself and cause inner conflict.

Another example is an older woman who has poor self-esteem from unresolved childhood issues. She tries to build herself up by dressing like a sexy, youthful 'hottie'. Every time a man pays her attention that satisfies her image of *'I'm sexy'*, she experiences a temporary emotional boost. This thrill overrides the anxiety and worry caused by her misconception, *'I'm not good enough as I am'*. The youthful 'hottie' image also succeeds at separating the woman from the deep sadness that remains buried from her childhood, making it much harder to identify and heal.

Self-images can be positive or negative. But even when an image is 'positive', it will prohibit emotional growth if it's preventing expression from your real self. When you project from an image, you detach from your *authentic* feelings. You're no longer connected to your true self.

Discovering Your Self-Images

Although invisible to the human eye, self-images can be identified through your self-discovery process. For example, during one of your meditations, you may ask why you are feeling so defensive. Seconds later, the answer may appear by 'seeing' a wall or some other barrier in your mind's eye. If you take it a step further, you may 'look' behind the wall and notice a much younger version of yourself — as a frightened child curled up in a corner. Or some other contracted figure that is unwilling to 'be seen' or partake in life.

Another clue is self-images don't grow up. They exist in the time frame when they were originally created. You may be surprised to learn that many of your current behaviors are driven by self-images that you created a very long time ago. Buried in the recesses of your unconscious mind, you remain unaware of why you still do some of the things you do. Even though you consciously don't want to!

Self-images are subjective in nature. They often project your personal biases as the 'entire picture', leaving no room for other considerations. There are several types of images that can block your authentic self-expression. For example, you may have a 'pious' image of yourself within your church group, an 'aggressive' self-image at work, or a 'loving spouse' self-image at home. Try to identify when you're coming from your real self vs. when you're acting from a manufactured, self-image. As you recognize the difference, you can opt to share only your authentic expressions.

Dissolving Images

A general overview of childhood experiences is not enough to dissolve an image. Self-images are dissolved by identifying the misconceptions that keep them 'alive'. Once you're aware of a self-image, become curious. What made you create this image? What belief is maintaining it? Then challenge your belief - is it true? What would happen if you let it go? Are you willing to feel and release your feelings? This healing process provides a direct opening to your spiritual mind and accesses vital energy flow. As you understand why you created your self-images, you bring yourself into present time. Without dissolving or at least becoming aware of them, emotional and spiritual growth will unnecessarily stagnate.

*Know your images and work daily and diligently to dissolve them.
They are the gatekeepers that prevent entrance to your inner Kingdom.*

When feelings are truthfully expressed and released, they are set free to merge with the eternal life force that is also within you. Tapping into the high-voltage energy of universal source *within* propels, strengthens and prepares you for constructive living. You become compatible with the nature of change instead of fearing it. You become prepared to willingly adapt to and make room for all the foreseeable and unforeseeable changes that life presents.

Dimming Your Light?

If you grew up with parents (or other primary caregivers) who openly acknowledged that your feelings were important and worthy, you're one of a privileged few. Family upbringing, culture, and environment contribute greatly to the development of personal belief systems. If you weren't taught how to effectively communicate your emotions, you probably did your best to avoid, hide, squash or bury them. Feelings can be frightening if you haven't learned how to rely on the strength of your spiritual mind. You may not know that your spiritual self is strong enough to hold you steady while your feelings flow through you, even the 'bad' ones.

When unpleasant feelings are avoided and suppressed, they take on a life of their own. No matter how deeply buried, feelings can and still do reach you. In your state of fear and ignorance, you don't seek guidance and protection from your spiritual mind. Instead, you seek it from your fear-filled state. Fear can't produce anything but more of itself. So any solution produced from your fearful state will be riddled with uncertainty and leave you feeling insecure. This is where hard, defensive attitudes are born. To protect yourself, you think: *'I don't care'*, *'I didn't want him/her anyway'*, *'What I have to say doesn't matter so I won't bother to communicate at all'*.

While your defensive, painful convictions remain within, your spiritual mind gets pushed further and further away. You confuse your child-like defense mechanisms with true power. You misconstrue stubbornness and anger as strength; sassiness as confidence; aggression as assertion; force as power. Arguing and one-upmanship are incorrectly viewed as the only way to 'win'. As more time passes, you begin to believe that you are your defenses. You detach from your true self as you pledge allegiance to your defenses. You are no longer capable of detecting what is real. Cruelty and separation become habitual behaviors. All for the sake of maintaining your so-called 'safety'. Distance becomes an illusory necessity, even from the people you admire. Even from the people you still want to love and wish to be close to, so very deep down.

> *"Truly, I say to you, unless you turn and become like children, you will never enter the kingdom of heaven."*
>
> *Matthew 18:3*

Letting Go

Defense mechanisms keep your self-images alive. They wouldn't have any power if you stopped defending their existence. But letting go of your 'safety-guards' can be difficult if they're all you've ever known. These strong, personal convictions that hold your self-image(s) intact feel very real. They may even make you feel powerful. Not having them to fall back on can make you feel unsafe and unprotected. So you hold on and remain stuck in old, unproductive ways instead of mourning the death of your so-called 'protectors'.

Letting go of your defensive behavior becomes much easier once you learn how to align with your spiritual self. You may not know who or what your spiritual self is. Initially, you may doubt Its presence. Or, you may not be ready to heed Its advice. For instance, you may have created a 'victim' image of yourself within your family unit. If you try to abandon this particular identity, you may suddenly feel threatened. Negative self-chatter may try to trick you into believing that you are abandoning your family. Or that they will leave you if you change and become 'all that'.

Even when you consciously believe that dissolving a negative image will be beneficial to your overall health, you may still feel challenged. Why? Because your self-image doesn't know there's somewhere greater to go. It has separated and strayed too far from your true self. Instead, it bullies, whines, cries, complains and moans to get its way. The mindset of an image can be very stubborn and often refuses to be accountable. It's basically very lazy and doesn't want any responsibility. This part of yourself has no problem with using, abusing, lying or cheating to get what it wants. But remember that although this part of you has separated from your spiritual self, it's still your mind. So you get to choose what you will and will not think.

*Words have been used for centuries to mask feelings,
but the energy of those words can't be disguised.*

Turn Your Light Up!

As you develop self-awareness and grow emotionally, you will begin to recognize many self-images. While you work toward dissolving your images, you can still experience peace and calm. One of the quickest ways to feel better during your self-discovery process is to be present – emotionally, mentally, physically, and spiritually.

Presence offers you the option to perceive objectively. When you fully experience present time, you are free to separate yourself from emotional triggers. You are free to listen and receive insight and clarity from your true self. You can objectively challenge the misconceptions of your images without feeling threatened. You can contemplate more current, practical considerations. For example, let's say you created a self-image of unworthiness. While being present, you can objectively challenge whether you are as imperfect and unworthy as your image projects. Or, if you created a 'perfect' image of yourself, you can examine whether you are as 'perfect' as your self-created image professes you to be.

In your state of presence, you can identify what is real and release what isn't. Pain and sadness is no longer a threat. You can see the original pain as it really is. It doesn't have to be exaggerated or dramatized. The despair that at one time seemed unbearable becomes simply another feeling that is processed through your energy system. Here in the now, you know that it can't devastate you.

Being present reconnects you with the strength and wisdom of your spiritual self. Your memories remain, but your images and the painful lies you concluded about yourself dissolve. And so do your images. You may still have sadness about something in the past, but genuine feelings are real. Any feeling that is real is compatible with the eternal life force that is also real, allowing emotional energy to move through you and be healed by such a pure source.

Presence also sharpens your reason and will centers. You can objectively identify the state of consciousness from which you are perceiving – Child? Defense? Self-Image? Spiritual? Being present reveals the true nature of your emotional biases. You are afforded the opportunity to reflect and realign if necessary, before choosing an action. With a focused and strong mind, emotional deterrents can no longer divert you from the present moment.

Objectivity is an important part of the maturation process. The more you mature, the more objective you become. Your needy demand for attention and approval subsides. Your childish desire to be front and center evaporates. You are courageous enough to accept all of your emotions, even the feelings you'd rather not sense, feel, or admit to yourself. Vicious cycles of pandemonium cease and desist. Compassion and understanding begin to fill you instead.

You create self-images to receive love,
but you won't be fulfilled unless you give love.

Splits and Breaks in Present Time

"The more you do, the more valued you are" is a well-known motto in corporate culture. Really? Let's rethink this. If your thoughts are splitting off and going in several different directions, your mind and body are out of sync. Multi-tasking prevents you from being present. Dividing your attention fragments your energy and actually weakens you. So stop. Pause and breathe. Check in with your divine intelligence before your thoughts begin to split off. Sit still and quietly pose the following question to your inner being, "What is the best approach I can take today to complete all of my responsibilities?" Then settle in until you reach the calm within yourself. Accept the instructive guidance of your spiritual self that already knows what's best for you. Align with the highest within yourself, and you will achieve what's best for you, and for those around you.

Spirit doesn't work. It doesn't do. It is.

Exercises to quickly bring yourself into present time

Pranayama Breathing

Pranayama breathing is an excellent yoga technique to calm and bring yourself into present time quickly. There are several different types of Pranayama, but the one below is 3-3-3-3.

To begin, sit in a comfortable position and start to observe your breath. Once you're aware of your breathing rhythm, start counting up to 3 as you inhale, as you exhale, and in between each breath:

Count up to 3 as you inhale.

Hold and count up to 3.

Exhale as you count up to 3.

Hold as you count up to 3.

Inhale as you count up to 3.

Hold as you count up to 3.

Exhale as you count up to 3.

Hold as you count up to 3.

Continue with this practice for 3 minutes. (You can use the timer on your phone to keep time.)

'I AM' Meditation

The purpose of the 'I AM' meditation is to develop enough self-awareness so you can objectively differentiate between your genuine feelings and emotional reactions.

Some practice is necessary to first learn how to observe and later control your thought process. This meditation will not take much time at all during each sitting, but a routine practice is necessary to align with the 'I AM' observer state.

1. Sit down at least twice a day for five minutes, not more, any time you wish (morning, afternoon or evening); do not lie down.
2. Relax without trying to exert any force, strain, or pressure.
3. Begin to follow the abdominal movements of your breath when you breathe; up and down, up and down.
4. Your mind will soon be disrupted by involuntary thoughts. Expect them, observe them quietly. While observing, capture your thoughts in precise terms. For example, *"I'm worrying I'm planning, I'm fantasizing"* and gently return to focusing on your breath. Be sure that you don't rehash the entire scene or situation that you're observing. That will waste mental energy.

- If your thoughts are not of pressing importance, just let them go and return to following your breath.
- If they are significant and something you need to look at, you can:
  - note to analyze them after your 5-minute meditation
  - or, if they are very pressing, you can work with them in the moment

EXERCISE

Dissolving Images and Energy Blocks through a Daily Record

Maintaining a daily record of personal interactions will help you develop awareness of your images and distortions. This doesn't have to take a lot of time. Ten to fifteen minutes at the end of each day should do it. Or you can take a few minutes throughout the day. You only need to write down a word or two. Words or phrases that will help you track behavioral patterns that are not aligned with your spiritual self. Over time, you will notice a pattern. You may not immediately recognize or understand your distortions that are causing inner turmoil. But don't give up. Through self-awareness and re-education, you will be able to access more of your spiritual self. During your daily review, be sure to set your intention to confront any shame or other uncomfortable feelings that may arise. Internal growth is a slow process. Pray for the courage to accept what you're not able to immediately change while acknowledging it.

> *God, grant me the serenity to accept the things I cannot change,*
> *the courage to change the things that I can,*
> *and the wisdom to know the difference.*
>
> *Reverend Reinhold Niebuhr*

Below are questions you can ask yourself in your daily self-discovery process. They will help you identify hidden beliefs and attitudes that are not aligned with your spiritual self:

1. What is the incident or relationship that is causing you discomfort or stress?

2. Pray for the strength and insight to help you connect this outer situation with the inner attitude that is attracting this situation toward you.

3. Write down all of your attitudes that may be keeping you 'stuck' in pain and discomfort. (Make a note if there are any personal biases or an unwillingness to let go on your part.)

4. Write down any and all negative attitudes that are justifying your defenses.

5. Do your responses remind you of any familiar, repeated patterns in your childhood?

6. Once you identify the misconception or distortion that is holding your image in place, clarify and replace it with the truth. This will bring you into present time.

7. Instruct your conscious mind to direct your thoughts and actions in a positive direction.

8. Pray for the strength and courage to help you move in this new direction.

9. To the best of your ability, try to see this same situation from the other person's perspective. Pretend you are in their shoes and explain the situation from their point of view.

Psychological issues are spiritual issues.

PART TWO

SPIRITUAL TRANSFORMATION

21 SPIRITUAL LAWS FROM THE PATHWORK GUIDE LECTURES

"The Kingdom of God Is *Within* You."

Luke 17:21

21 SPIRITUAL LAWS

In this section, you will find twenty one spiritual laws summarized from the Pathwork lectures. Each law contains valuable information for your spiritual transformation process. No law is considered more important than another. Exercises are provided after each law to embody and experience them in a deep and personal way. For additional learning, you can also download any of the Pathwork lectures for free @ www.pathwork.org.

The goal of each exercise is to open the channel to your spiritual mind. Developing a clear channel takes time, patience and perseverance. Don't rush through your practice. Give yourself the necessary time for reflection. The amount of time you will need to reflect on each question may vary. Feel free to repeat the exercises as often as necessary. You don't have to proceed through the laws in alphabetical order as they are laid out here. You can flip through and read those that are most appropriate and are 'speaking' to you in the moment.

A routine practice of each exercise will increase your ability to intuit with clarity. Pray and ask for support to help you build an inner bridge to your spirit. Your spiritual guides are always available. Don't be afraid to ask for help.

The spiritual laws can serve as meaningful discussions to have with your family and friends. If possible, try to do the exercises together. Honest, important conversations often lead to strong, supportive networks.

One last note: Prayer is suggested in many of the exercises. If you're uncomfortable with praying, or simply have forgotten how to pray, you might want to skip ahead and first read 'The Spiritual Law of Prayer'.

*The thoughts you think are yours. You think them,
and therefore you can choose to change them.*

CONTENTS

21 Spiritual Laws

Abundance	40
Acceptance	43
Balance	47
Brotherhood and Sisterhood	51
Commitment	56
Compatibility	60
Free Will	63
Happiness	66
Love	70
Magnetism	73
Mobility	77
Mutuality	80
Peace	83
Perfection	86
Prayer	89
Presence	94
Relaxation	97
Responsibility	100
Surrender	103
Truth	106
Unity	109

THE SPIRITUAL LAW OF ABUNDANCE

Abundance comes from knowing that you are a part of the infinite, universal source.

> *"I will not say that the universal spirit is in you, I say that you are it."*
>
> The Guide, Pathwork Lecture #175
> 'Consciousness'

Surrendering to the abundant being that you already are requires courage, trust, and faith. Imaginary threats may twist the truth and exaggerate potentially bad outcomes, but that is fear talking.

Every time you give energy to your fear-based thoughts, you weaken the powerful, creative thought-forms that are already working toward fulfilling your desires. Fear redirects your energy and pulls you into the opposite direction. Your intention for fulfillment loses traction and successful outcomes are further delayed.

Whenever there is a lack of abundance in any area of your life, look within for self-sabotaging thoughts. Fear is always the culprit. It wants to keep you small and your life mundane. A daily routine of self-observation will keep your fear in check. When you identify the voice of fear, re-educate it. Allow your conscious mind to repeat this universal truth: "I AM a part of the eternal life force that can never die".

Expect lasting fulfillment when you identify with the truth of who you are. Fear is poor. You are not.

The Spiritual Law of Abundance

Summary

Anything created from the state of "I AM" consciousness is everlasting because it's aligned in truth – life is infinite abundance.

Abundance comes from knowing that you are a part of the infinite universal source that is full of limitless possibilities.

Surrendering to the abundant being that you already are requires courage, trust, and faith.

Every time you give energy to fear-based thoughts, you interfere with the strong thought-forms that are working toward fulfilling your desires

> *When the soul is sufficiently experienced and deeply impressed with the truth that there is nothing to fear, the human personality suddenly comes to a point of realization in which acceptance is no longer a risk, for it embraces the entire benign universe. Then it is no longer a question of having to go through the fear in order to rise above it. Then one is prepared for all the fulfillment, the abundance, the bliss and pleasure supreme in a liberated life, and in the life eternal, with all its dynamic, joyful aspects. All that the human heart desires is immediately available when one has overcome fear.*
>
> *- The Guide, Pathwork Lecture #130*
> *Finding True Abundance By Going Through Your Fear*

Realign With Your Spiritual Mind

Spiritual Law: Abundance

Violation: Fear

Violating Behaviors: Cheating, stealing, forcing, grabbing

Abundance Challenge

1. Write down something that you long for and your motivations for wanting it.

2. Observe and 'listen' for any fear you may have around not getting what you desire. Or, is there fear around getting what you want?

3. What happens when you imagine yourself 'letting go' of your fear?

4. Visualize yourself having what you want and feeling fulfilled. Try to maintain the positive feeling for as long and as often as you can while you're working toward achieving your desire.

Thoughts to Think

"There are many unknown elements in my life. I will no longer try to control what I cannot. I remain open and expect positive experiences to flow through and to me."

THE SPIRITUAL LAW OF ACCEPTANCE

Self-acceptance relaxes the physical body and allows life force to flow freely.

When the mind is open and the body is relaxed, an inner pathway opens and releases powerful life force energy. This healing force permeates all levels of your being, strengthening a deep sense of interconnectedness within.

Peace is not attainable without total acceptance. For instance, even though you may have *intellectually* accepted a difficult situation, you may still feel *emotionally* unsettled due to lingering feelings such as resentment, hatred or jealousy. Accepting all of your emotions, including feelings you don't like, will allow you to relax. The wisdom of your spiritual mind will become readily accessible. Understanding will come to you.

Helpful insights from deep within will shine light on the root cause of your outer disturbances. For example, let's say you're faced with having to confront someone about a bothersome situation. Self-acceptance will relax you enough so you can recognize your own defensive attitudes that are likely contributing to the problem. Negative attitudes such as:

Pride: "I will appear wrong and weak if (she/he) proves to be right."

Self-will: "My way is the only way. I refuse to consider (his/her) opinion."

Fear: "I'll be ridiculed or I will lose if I open up". "It's too risky to be myself."

Emotional defenses only separate you from inner peace and calm. The intelligence of your spiritual mind is a loving resource that is available to you, and to all of those around you - when you're open enough to receive it. All you need is the courage to accept yourself as you truly are.

The Spiritual Law of Acceptance

Summary

Self-acceptance relaxes the physical body allowing life force to flow freely.

Accepting yourself as you are now, including all of your conflicting emotions, will free the wisdom of your spiritual mind.

Self-acceptance will relax you enough so you can recognize your defensive attitudes, such as:

Pride: "I will appear weak and wrong if she/he is right"

Self-will: "My way is the only way"

Fear: "I'll be ridiculed if I dare to be myself"

"The true and right course to accept life's adversities is: 'I expect life to bring me unhappiness as well as happiness. I will not flinch from life's clouds. I will not fear the darkness. Only by going through adversity courageously will I be able to bear happiness and be able to give happiness.' If you learn from the hard times and ask God in your darkest hour what it is that He wants you to learn and what it is in you that has caused misfortune to come to you, then you have the right attitude ... Another distortion of a divine attribute concerns dignity. Dignity is a divine aspect. Its distortion is pride ... In the measure that self-will, pride, vanity, and egotism are present in the soul, they inevitably bring fear in their wake."

- The Guide, Pathwork Lecture #37
Acceptance, Right and Wrong Way – Dignity in Humility

Realign With Your Spiritual Mind

Spiritual Law: Acceptance

Violation: Self-rejection

Violating Behaviors: Compulsion, denial, envy, jealousy, obsession, perfectionism

Acceptance Challenge

1. Write down a situation (or relationship) that you have trouble accepting in your life.

2. Identify your attitudes and beliefs that prevent you from accepting this situation.

3. Does this situation reflect a lack of acceptance in yourself?

4. Identify and record any of your 'lower' character traits such as vanity, stubbornness, etc. that are preventing you from accepting the situation (or relationship).

Thoughts to Think

"I humbly accept all parts of myself including the mental, emotional, physical and spiritual aspects of my being. I will not judge myself or others. Instead of masking or avoiding any pain or discomfort, I will accept it and explore the root cause of its existence."

THE SPIRITUAL LAW OF BALANCE

To the degree you're willing to merge your spiritual mind with your outer mind, to that degree will you experience peace, calm, and creativity.

The wisdom of your spiritual mind perceives what your outer mind can't. Your spiritual self intuits and responds to the rhythm of your inner clock. It senses and registers all of your desires and real needs. It knows how to support you in fulfilling your daily responsibilities. Your higher mind knows when it's best to work and play; and when to rest and be receptive.

When the spiritual mind is not present, your thoughts can quickly transition to worry, frustration, anxiety or exhaustion. This distressful state can easily be avoided by accessing the wisdom of your spiritual self. A commitment to daily devotion and prayer will unite the innate intelligence of your divine mind with the faculties of your outer mind. As you create inner harmony and outer balance, you also fulfill a much greater task. You begin to recognize areas of your consciousness that is still stuck in distortion. You have the opportunity to restore and reconnect truth to the disconnected parts of yourself. Through this self-integration process, you'll notice a decline of negativity and chaos within, around and about you.

The Spiritual Law of Balance

Summary

Your spiritual mind knows exactly what you need to nurture yourself.

Balance is often associated with only the outer functions of daily life: work, play, rest, and sleep.

Relying entirely on your outer functions causes much distress, exhaustion and anxiety.

Daily devotion to your spiritual self through meditation and emotional development will unite the inner wisdom of your spiritual mind with the faculties of your outer mind.

> *"This inner center is the divine consciousness. It permeates the entire universe, it comprises all. Hence, the inner center of each human being is one with the inner center of every other human being. All are filled with the living unity that knows no conflict and no limitation. The creative power at work in any life process is all one and the same. The separation of matter and consciousness is illusion. This illusion is the real meaning of what religion refers to as separation from God, or the "Fall of the Angels". The state of bliss that results from working oneself back to integration and contact with the inner center is the goal not only of this path but, on an unconscious level, of every living being."*
>
> *- The Guide, Pathwork Lecture #137*
> *Balance of Inner and Outer Control*

Realign With Your Spiritual Mind

Spiritual Law: Balance

Violation: Identification with inferior and superior self-images

Violating Behaviors: Anxiety, avoidance, agitation, dramatization, exaggeration, self-denial, weariness

Balance Challenge

Set aside time each day for approximately 15 minutes to meditate and develop self-awareness.

1. Sit in silence and observe any areas within where you feel tension or discomfort.

2. Call upon the wisdom of your spiritual self and ask, "What is the root cause of my discomfort?"

3. Be open and allow yourself to receive an answer from your spiritual mind. You may not receive an immediate response. Don't worry! Be patient and use your mind to imagine a positive solution – even if it doesn't feel real. Expecting positive possibilities can become a wonderful habit.

4. Be patient. You are learning how to align with your spiritual voice and its power. This is a noble task that requires effort and perseverance.

Thoughts to Think

"I am willing to meditate each day and allow the wisdom of my spiritual mind to blend with the intellect of my outer mind. I allow Spirit to guide, inspire, and move through me."

THE SPIRITUAL LAW OF BROTHERHOOD AND SISTERHOOD

The willingness to present your true self to another person strengthens the connection to your spiritual self.

Meaningful communication is the result of positive intention. Others can sense your intention through their own higher self perception. The true self registers integrity, regardless of how self-aware you or they are. As the authentic sender, you offer the receiver the gift of your integrity and dignity. In return, you experience the warmth of your own authenticity. When you have the courage to be yourself, you remain open and connected to the power and love of truth. You are free to focus on what you really want instead of busying yourself for the sake of appearances and outer approval.

Recommitting to the truth within yourself each day, even hourly, creates an opening to deeper knowing. As you willingly expose the truth of who you are, *no matter how scary that may seem at first,* you also dissolve weak character traits. For example:

- ❖ Pride shrivels to the degree you refuse to appear better *or less* than others
- ❖ Self-will vanishes when you stop blaming others for your own discomfort and negativity
- ❖ Fear of rejection disappears as your true self proves to be enough

Technology has made communication much easier to superficially connect with others, but technological devices are not an excuse for inauthenticity. As the sender, you will receive whatever you put out. That is the law.

The Spiritual Law of Brotherhood and Sisterhood

Summary

Meaningful communication is the result of positive intention.

Others can sense your intention through their own higher self perception.

Recommitting to the truth within your self creates an opening to deeper knowing.

The willingness to present your true self to another person strengthens the connection to your spiritual self.

> *"Each thought of hate, of separation, of egoism, of injustice, of discrimination, of wanting more for oneself than for one's neighbor, in short, each thought that breaks God's laws, is a building block in that enormous spiritual structure – war – which must first be formed in spirit before it can manifest destruction on the material plane. If only a small part of humankind sowed the seeds of peace, wars would not exist, in spite of a few unscrupulous politicians. Most people, including you, my friends, harbor thoughts of anxiety, and if not thoughts of hate, then of mistrust and separation, such as between one group and another – and all these violate the law of brotherhood [and sisterhood]. Each thought of this kind, each emotion is a significant contribution to the outbreak of war."*
>
> *- The Guide, Pathwork Lecture # 12*
> *The Order and Diversity of the Spiritual Worlds –*
> *The Process of Reincarnation*

Realign With Your Spiritual Mind

Spiritual Law: Brotherhood and Sisterhood

Violation: Separation

Violating Behaviors: Envy, backstabbing, maligning, sarcasm, self-righteousness, withdrawal

Brotherhood/Sisterhood Challenge

1. List a fault and/or weakness that you try to hide from others.

2. What behaviors do you exhibit to hide this fault? What feelings are you unwilling to expose so they can heal? Why?

3. Identify the arrogance within yourself that states you should be better than you currently are. Write down what it specifically says.

4. Each day, pray for the strength to see yourself as you truly are without judgment.

5. Visualize and imagine what your authentic self is without this fault. Allow this image of your true self to form in your mind's eye. Call upon and visit with the image of your true self often throughout each day.

Thoughts to Think

"I will make a conscious, continual effort to authentically articulate and communicate with others. If my conversations are too limiting, unclear, or defensive, I will ask in meditation to receive the wisdom about the root cause of my discomfort. I will follow the spiritual guidance I receive to dissolve it."

THE SPIRITUAL LAW OF COMMITMENT

Commitment is driven by spirited willpower, undivided attention, and positive, personal investment.

When you are fully committed to an endeavor, relationship, cause, or any large or small task, your spiritual self is actively engaged. Commitment is a whole-hearted effort complete with persistent focus and drive. It involves all of your faculties including your mental capacity, physical capability, and emotional willingness.

If you're not feeling fully committed to an endeavor, look for a negative intention. Ask yourself:

"Am I giving it my best shot?"
"Am I completely focused?"
"Is there a part of me that doesn't want to give?"
"Am I being totally honest with myself?"

Negative intentions are often buried within the unconscious and cause shame. By confronting yourself with honest questions, you are guaranteed answers. You will receive insights about why you aren't entirely motivated. An honest self-evaluation will help you understand, re-assess and re-commit to your goals. As you acknowledge your unwillingness, you can re-align, redirect and see yourself through to completion.

Self-honesty will help you build a solid, inner platform. As you stand on firm inner footing, you can manifest your dreams and achieve your goals.

The Spiritual Law of Commitment

Summary

Commitment is driven by spirited willpower, undivided attention, and positive, personal investment.

By confronting yourself with honest questions, you can identify negativity that prevents you from achieving your goals.

Acknowledging an 'inner no' to your conscious yes will help you re-focus and re-commit.

Self-honesty will help you build a solid inner platform that you can stand on and manifest your dreams.

> *"Commitment means, above all, a one-pointedness of attention; giving the self in a wholehearted way to whatever the commitment may be. If you are committed to give your best to whatever you do, you will focus on all aspects of the subject. You will not shy away from investing all your energies, all your attention. You will use your faculties of thinking, of intuition, of meditation. In other words, you will use your physical energies, your mental capacities, your feelings, and your will to activate the as yet dormant spiritual powers to make the venture constructive. This requires a holistic approach that can come only when the will is unbroken by negative counterforces. In order to be fully committed, no negative intentionality must exist."*
>
> *- The Guide, Pathwork Lecture # 196*
> *Commitment: Cause and Effect*

Realign With Your Spiritual Mind

Spiritual Law: Commitment

Violation: Negative intentions

Violating Behaviors: Apathy, excuses, laziness, inertia, negativity, stagnation

Commitment Challenge

1. Identify an area in your life where you have difficulty committing yourself to a relationship, project, or a situation.

2. Write down all the reasons why you are not fulfilling your commitment.

3. Do you recognize any negative intention(s) that is preventing you from making a full commitment? If so, what is it?

4. Are you aware of the pain your negative intention is causing you and/or others? If so, are you willing to admit your feelings of guilt for the pain that you are intentionally causing?

5. Align with the power and intelligence of your spiritual mind. Re-state your positive intention about your commitment, including the sincere desire to let go of any negative intention.

Thoughts to Think

"I commit to fully engage in my relationships with others. This includes acknowledging and consciously giving up my negative intentions and spiteful withholdings."

THE SPIRITUAL LAW OF COMPATIBILITY

Your spiritual self is already compatible with the eternal life force. You can feel this immense, benign power when your thoughts and behaviors are aligned with your divine intentions.

When 'I' is considered more important than 'we', an energetic split occurs within your psyche. You separate yourself from the unified state. Other dualistic thoughts such as either/or, good/bad, winner/loser also contribute to this inner division. Whenever you are presented with a dualistic choice of 'me' vs. 'them', ask your spiritual self for advice on how to establish 'we' consciousness. The spiritual mind is inclusive and always considers everyone involved. It will provide you with the universal perspective.

Every time you dissolve a negative belief, you become more compatible with your spiritual self in the unified state. Be persistent when you summon your inner divinity. Inspiration communicates in many forms. Be ready. Expect to be fulfilled. Expect to receive answers. Expect obstacles to vanish as you identify more and more with your spiritual being.

The spirit of truth is available to you *always*.

The Spiritual Law of Compatibility

Summary

The power of your spiritual self becomes a live, feeling reality when your thoughts and behaviors are compatible with your divine intentions.

Whenever you are presented with a divisive choice such as *'me vs. them'*, ask your spiritual self to help you identify an inclusive solution that establishes *'we'* consciousness.

Every time you dissolve a negative belief, you become more compatible with your spiritual mind.

"Your compatibility with life lies in trusting it and building on this trust; in knowing that it is unlimited and that it brings forth exactly according to your expectation, attitude, and concept. The firmer this conviction becomes as you repeatedly experience this truth, the more trustful, relaxed, positive, creative and generous you become."

- The Guide, Pathwork Lecture # #179
Chain Reactions In the Dynamics of Creative Life Substance

Realign With Your Spiritual Mind

Spiritual Law: Compatibility

Violation: Duality; internal split causing disunity within your beliefs, attitudes, and opinions

Violating Behaviors: Bullying, backstabbing, deceit, dishonesty, double-dealing, two-faced

Compatibility Challenge

1. Identify a situation where you perceive yourself as being any of the following: the loser or winner; right or wrong; good or bad.

2. Write down all of your personal beliefs about what it means to perceive yourself as both (i.e. wrong and right).

3. Imagine yourself as a pure, spiritual being. Then review your answers in question #2 from this unified state. If necessary, pray for help to receive objective responses that are compatible with universal truth. (Note: If you notice resistance, write it down as that is an objective observation of a subjective feeling.)

Thoughts to Think

"I know that there are more than two options available for any situation. I open myself up to receive the intelligence and wisdom of my spiritual self. I invite this part of myself to inspire and harmonize all of my relationships."

THE SPIRITUAL LAW OF FREE WILL

The will of your spiritual mind is the same as God's will for you – complete happiness and total fulfillment in all areas of your life.

Free will grants you the generous gift of choice. You are free to choose your thoughts, emotions, actions, reactions and behaviors. Since free will is a spiritual law, God will not intervene in your decision making unless you extend an invitation.

You can always identify the will of your spiritual self by its tone, 'feel', and location. The rays that deliver your spiritual messages emanate from the area of your solar plexus where the spiritual magnetic field is located. These soft and consistent messages travel through the mental and emotional subtle bodies until reaching the outer regions of your physical body and beyond.

Your outer mind also has a will of its own, which is often at odds with the intentions of your spiritual mind. You can easily recognize thoughts that are driven solely by your outer intellect by a lack of inner calm. When you're feeling restless, look no further than to the motives of your 'lower' self. Negativity not only steals your peace, but produces tension, pressure and friction with others as well.

If you should happen to notice that you're willing your power in two opposing directions, pause. Once you slow yourself down enough, you can identify the origin of your thoughts and motives. As you reflect, you can choose to focus only on what's best and move forward with positive, clear intention.

The power is yours. Choose wisely.

The Spiritual Law of Free Will

Summary

The will of your spiritual self is the same as God's will for you.

You are free to choose your thoughts, emotions, actions, reactions and behaviors.

Since free will is a spiritual law, God will not intervene unless you extend an invitation.

When you're feeling restless, look no further than to the motives of your 'lower' self.

> *"God has created the Universe, which is governed by an infinite number of laws. He created His children and gave them free will so they could choose to keep or not to keep the laws long before this earth and this material world came into existence. The keeping of these laws entails happiness, love, harmony, light, and supreme wisdom, because God, who is perfect, cannot create anything but perfection. Yet, if any creature were to be forced to stay within the framework of these laws, as if they had no free will, the laws would neither be what they are, nor would they be in accordance with the nature of God."*
>
> *- The Guide, Pathwork Lecture #18*
> *Free Will*

Realign With Your Spiritual Mind

Law: Free Will

Violation: Domination

Violating Behaviors: Control, manipulation, subordination, submission, victimization

Free Will Challenge

1. List all the successes in your life where you have had tremendous progress and outcomes. List as many as you would like.

2. What choices did you make to produce such satisfactory results?

3. Think of a situation where you tried to force or manipulate someone or some situation to get your own way (no matter how subtle).

4. Identify the error in your thought process that made you think you had to be manipulative or forceful.

5. By not aligning with the highest intention within yourself, what price did you pay?

Thoughts to Think

"I choose happiness, fulfillment and peace by aligning with the will of my spiritual self which is also the will of God."

THE SPIRITUAL LAW OF HAPPINESS

As you offer your inherent gifts and talents to others, you fulfill the law of happiness by serving as a meaningful spoke in the wheel of life.

If you don't know what your natural God-given gifts are, pause for a moment and take a personal inventory of your talents and assets. It may be that you have a strong, supportive family that you can rely upon. You may be intellectually gifted, or have access to well-connected networks of people. You may be in great shape and enjoy good health. You may have any or all of the above.

God knows the sincerity of your heart. If you sincerely desire to be a conduit for joy, you will receive spiritual guidance on how to proceed. Opportunities will appear.

Meditate to discover how much of what you want is truly for others or just for yourself. Be honest in your self-search. Consider it a positive step if you discover a self-serving attitude. Such awareness is an opportunity for growth. The new knowledge of your self-discovery can help you realign any intention that doesn't serve your highest good.

A daily practice of positive intention-setting will create strong, eternal, spiritual thought-forms.

The Spiritual Law of Happiness

Summary

As you offer your inherent gifts to others, you contribute happiness to humanity.

God knows the sincerity of your heart.

The spiritual law of happiness is fulfilled when you give to others what is naturally bestowed to you.

Discovering a self-serving attitude is an opportunity for growth.

A daily practice of positive intention-setting will create strong, eternal, spiritual thought-forms.

> *"…think about what particular blessings you enjoy; it may be good health, or spiritual strength, or the happiness and security of a loving relationship; it is different with each one of you. Everybody has received a special treasure from God. And once you have decided, 'I will no longer want to be the ultimate goal, but rather a link in the chain,' it will be shown to you how you can pass on that which you have received, and you will be rewarded, for that is the law."*
>
> *- The Guide, Pathwork Lecture # 5*
> *Happiness for Yourself or Happiness As a Link in the Chain of Life*

Realign With Your Spiritual Mind

Spiritual Law: Happiness

Violation: Selfishness, Ignorance

Violating Behaviors: Agitation, anxiety, complacency, depression, dissatisfaction, repression

Happiness Challenge

The following exercise will help you commit to developing your inner strength.

1. Identify an area in your life where you have difficulty maintaining happiness, the feeling of positive, constructive life force flowing freely from and to you.

2. Are you aware of any painful feelings that you may be resisting? If so, what are they and why do you resist feeling them?

3. Write down what your inherent talents and gifts are that you can share with others. If you don't know, take the necessary time to pray and ask to be shown in your meditation.

4. Do you believe that you deserve to be happy? In a brief summary, write down the reasons why (This exercise applies to all answers: yes, no, maybe, in some cases, etc.).

5. Pray and ask how you can share your natural gifts and talents.

Thoughts to Think

"I choose to be a link in the evolving chain of happiness. I willingly share my inherent gifts and talents with those who wish to receive them. My goal is to be an instrument for happiness. I trust that my spiritual mind will provide me with the necessary guidance and wisdom."

THE SPIRITUAL LAW OF LOVE

Love gives because it needs to share. Love is the binding force that mends, bends, blends, protects and delivers good whenever and wherever it's allowed. You know this about love. You can sense it. You want to experience more of it and sometimes wonder why you can't or won't.

Is it doubt that stands in your way?

Do you know that you are worthy of such perfect health? Yes, love is health. Think about how your body functions in this heightened positive state. Your circulatory, digestive, nervous, muscular and endocrine systems function better. You feel more alive. You can see, hear, taste, feel and perceive more fully. This is the beauty and intelligence of love.

The willingness to love is a choice. And so is numbness. It's impossible to love if you're not willing to feel. The ability to exude warm, loving peace and kindness is entirely up to you. These sensations don't just happen *to* you. They must emanate *from* you.

Your aches represent the painful expressions of your sobbing soul. Your soul suffers when love is lacking in your life. It knows healthy connection and weeps when you're not there. Feed your soul by acknowledging and nurturing the love that exists within you. You may have to search for it at first – sometimes deeply, but find it. It's there waiting for you.

You can only give something you have and you can only draw toward you that which is already within you. That's the law.

The Spiritual Law of Love

Summary

Love gives because it needs to share.

The willingness to love is a choice. It's impossible to love if you're not willing to feel.

Love doesn't just happen to you. It must emanate from you.

You can only give something you have and you can only draw toward you that which is already within you.

Your soul knows healthy connection and weeps when you're not there.

> *"The love of the universe permeates all that is. It is always available, although often you are not aware of it because of the false direction of your thinking ... When you love, you remain in a state of health. It is obvious that love is a feeling, but it is not so obvious that this feeling must result from an act of will motivated by intelligence. So love is certainly intelligence ... Love is also much more than reason, will and emotion. It is sensation on every level of your being. When you are in a state of love, you see differently, you hear differently, you taste differently. Life around you has an altogether different flavor."*
>
> *- The Guide, Pathwork Lecture #240*
> *Aspects of the Anatomy of Love: Self-love, Structure, Freedom*

Realign With Your Spiritual Mind

Spiritual Law: Love

Violation: Self-hatred and self-loathing

Violating Behaviors: Bitterness, hate, misery, spite, stinginess, vanity; any type of mental, verbal, emotional, or physical abuse

Love Challenge

1. Record your emotional, mental, and physical responses when you are in a loving state.

2. When you feel agitated or perturbed, are you truly open and willing to consider a more positive feeling? Write down other thoughts and feelings that you can choose.

3. If you can't envision a more positive state, write down the reason(s) for any stubborn resistance or negative intention(s) you have that refuses good feelings.

4. What do your thoughts and reactions reflect about your own self-love (or lack of it)?

Thoughts to Think

"I have made mistakes and others have made mistakes. I admit that I have caused pain and I have received pain. I forgive myself and I forgive others. I acknowledge the spirit and dignity within myself to grow in love and truth."

THE SPIRITUAL LAW OF MAGNETISM

'Like attracts like' can easily be replaced with 'like magnetizes like'. 'Like attracts like' refers to the powerful magnetic force of thoughts and feelings and how together, they create strong magnetic fields.

Thought and energy are a continuum whereby each thought fuses with an energetic current and creates an electro-magnetic thought field or 'thought-form'. The magnetic properties of a thought-form attract people, relationships, and situations that have the same or similar energetic frequencies.

Your life experiences reflect the thought and energetic 'frequencies' of your own mind, including the deepest parts of your unconscious. Every belief, conviction, attitude, and opinion is fused with energetic strength and influence. You can always empower, restore or dissolve thought-forms with the electrifying vibration of truth.

If you are dissatisfied with a relationship or situation in your life, look within and find your own thought or attitude that magnetizes this situation toward you. Once you've identified the misconception that keeps you beholden to your unwanted situation, you can demagnetize it by replacing it with the truth. Your spiritual mind provides wise thoughts that resonate at high frequencies. The power of this pure energy source can dissolve the 'pull' that draws you toward unfulfilling outcomes. Without the energetic draw, you are free to walk away.

To access healing energies within, set your intention to align with your spiritual self. Ask for the wisdom, strength, and courage to dissolve any misconception that is causing destructive behaviors or unfulfilling relationships. The more you summon your inner divinity, the more effective you will be at demagnetizing all 'lower' self, destructive thought-forms. It takes time, patience and tenacity to identify inner thoughts that are producing dissatisfaction, but it's a search worth pursuing. It has eternal benefits.

Fill your mind with thoughts of your best self. See yourself as free, confident, ready, willing and able to participate fully in your life. The power of your thoughts is formidable. Think spiritually.

The Spiritual Law of Magnetism

Summary

"Like attracts like" can be replaced with "like magnetizes like".

Your life experiences reflect the thought and energetic 'frequencies' of your mind.

The power of truth can dissolve the energetic 'pull' that draws disappointing situations toward you.

The more you summon your inner divinity, the more effective you will be at demagnetizing all lower, destructive thought-forms.

> *"The fusion of consciousness and energy is of such a tremendous power that this fusion creates an electro-magnetic energy field, as it were. This field contains every conceivable seed, or possibility, of creation. Every conceivable attitude or concept about life creates such a force field. Once the force field is in action, it sets events, patterns, behavior, reactions, states of body and soul into its specific mold. The magnetism of this field is so strong that ensuing action and events are inexorably set in motion, and these actions and events continue to perpetuate the same power of this specific force field. The force field of a specific attitude to life is also ruled by laws of attraction — like attracting like. Thus you who have created various force fields as a result of your attitudes, ideas, concepts, and approaches to life attract or repulse events, people, happenings, actions of others and yourself."*
>
> - The Guide, Pathwork lecture # 201
> *Demagnetizing Negative Force Fields – Pain of Guilt*

Realign With Your Spiritual Mind

Spiritual Law: Magnetism

Violation: Alignment with negativity; attachment to misconceptions

Violating Behaviors: Aggression, defiance, greed, repulsion, vengefulness, willfulness

Magnetism Challenge

1. Sit in a comfortable position and call upon your inner divinity to help you center, be still and relax.

2. Allow every cell of your being to be filled with the truth of who you really are. Grant yourself permission to feel love.

3. Take an inventory and list all the good about your life. Write down your thoughts and attitudes that support all the good that you have.

4. Pray for the awareness, wisdom, and courage to change any beliefs that don't support your spiritual intentions and divine being.

Thoughts to Think

"Every thought is supported by powerful energy that creates a magnetic force field. I direct my willpower to create and sustain thoughts that are aligned with my highest intentions and spiritual truth."

THE SPIRITUAL LAW OF MOBILITY

In the unified state, everything is in harmonious, constant motion including your thoughts, beliefs, attitudes, and opinions.

Every time you think a thought, a movement is made. When you envision yourself receiving a promotion at work, winning a trophy, or sharing pleasurable moments with a loved one, your thoughts move through the sea of the universal energy field.

The movements of your mind contribute greatly to the outcome of your life's experiences. When your thoughts are positively aligned with universal truth, your body is fueled with feelings of warmth, calm, peace and rejuvenation. Personal biases are thought-forms 'stuck' in misconception. The energy of distortion doesn't flow freely and move forward. It's trapped in its own limited belief, circling round and round in a repeated pattern that goes nowhere. A thought-form mired in years of a particular belief creates sluggish movement or 'psychic paralysis'. Running in a blizzard storm can seem easier than trying to redirect such deeply ingrained, energetic grooves.

If you have difficulty maintaining happiness, identify the place and time that you chose not to feel good anymore. You may have unresolved childhood hurts that are continuing to spin in contracted states of fear. You could have pain that remains buried, stuck and unprocessed. If so, dig it out and move it forward into present time. Consult your spiritual mind for guidance if you're not sure how. This is a wonderful exercise for your soul.

The Spiritual Law of Mobility

Summary

In the unified state, everything is in harmonious, constant motion including your thoughts, beliefs, attitudes, and opinions.

Your thoughts move through the sea of the universal energy field.

Misconceptions cause thoughts to become trapped, moving aimlessly in circular, repeated patterns or in reverse motion.

The movements of your mind contribute greatly to your life's experiences.

> "The entire universe is permeated with a vibrant life substance … This tremendous life substance is in continuous motion … This substance consists of forces of such tremendous power that people have only begun to discover them vaguely and to a limited degree. Whether this power be physical, such as electrical or atomic power, or mental power makes no difference, for it is all the same power, or different facets of the same power. This power is a very impressionable mass, a substance that can be governed and molded only by consciousness."
>
> -The Guide, Pathwork Lecture # 135
> *Mobility in Relaxation – Suffering Through Attachment of the Life Force to Negative Situations*

Realign With Your Spiritual Mind

Spiritual Law: Mobility

Violation: Stagnation

Violating Behaviors: Apathy, depression, laziness, procrastination

Mobility Challenge

1. Observe one of your fantasies. It could be a wish or a daydream, something you would like to create in your life. Compare the fantasy with your reality.

2. Write down your pure, positive intention that mobilizes and supports your wish.

3. Record any negativity that interferes with your wish (i.e., pride, vanity, one-upmanship, etc.). When and why did you merge your life force with this negativity?

4. Connect with your spiritual self through meditation. Ask for help to release the pain that is maintaining your negative intention. Ask for guidance to make your fantasy become real and pure.

Thoughts to Think

"Life is in constant motion. My thoughts are in motion. I have the ability to direct my thoughts and energy in directions that are positive, healthy, and eternally lasting."

THE SPIRITUAL LAW OF MUTUALITY

Mutuality allows you to supersede your current state of existence. The relationship between your imagination that produces a creative idea and your willingness to execute it is a mutual agreement. When your imagination is supported by your willingness to execute, your creative ideas become tangible, physical manifestations. As a result, your personal power, strength, and creative ability flourishes. The successful outcome of any idea is evidence of mutual consent between your conscious and unconscious mind.

You may find it easier to fantasize about an idea than to execute it. When this happens, try to identify the 'no' in your subconscious mind that may be causing you to withdraw. As you identify misconceptions that hold you back, pause. Clarify and state the reason why your distorted belief doesn't justify your resignation. It could be that the necessary circumstances to manifest your idea are still in the gestation phase so you're 'in waiting'. Or, your spiritual gifts (and the ability to create is a spiritual gift) have lost their luster for an understandably good reason. But if fear or other negative intentions are causing you to freeze, you deserve to know this. Replace any unconscious misunderstanding with truth.

You don't have to look far for the wisdom of your spiritual mind, but you do have to admit when you say 'no' to it.

The Spiritual Law of Mutuality

Summary

Mutuality allows you to supersede your current state of existence.

When your imagination is supported by your willingness to execute, your creative ideas become tangible, physical manifestations.

You may find it easier to fantasize about an idea than to execute it.

You don't have to look far for the wisdom of your spiritual mind, but you do have to admit when you say 'no' to it.

> "The creative attitude is a free-flowing, spontaneous manifestation. Execution is an act that comes through the determination of the ego-will. It is more mechanical, more laborious and requires consistency and effort. This has totally different characteristics from the spontaneous, effortless influx of creative ideas. Human beings are uncreative for two reasons: either they are unwilling to adopt the necessary self-discipline to follow through on their creative ideas, or they are emotionally and spiritually too contracted to open their own individual creative channels. In the first case, they childishly refuse to be bothered by the difficulties, the trials and errors. In the second they lack inspiration. Both of these lopsided attitudes gradually balance themselves out when the individual grows on the path and begins to resolve his inner conflicts. The healthy, balanced person who has found himself always finds his personal creative outlet that yields the deepest satisfaction to his life."
>
> *- The Guide, Pathwork Lecture #185*
> *Mutuality – A Cosmic Principle and Law*

Realign With Your Spiritual Mind

Law: Mutuality

Violation: Rebellion

Violating Behaviors: Aggression, apathy, irritation, frustration, rage

Mutuality Challenge

1. Write down what you really want in your life.

2. Do you believe that you have done everything possible to achieve it?

3. Spiritualize your physical reality by filling yourself up with the energy of positive intention. Enhance the atmosphere of your home so it's divinely potent. Fill it with highly-energized, blessed-inspired creations.

4. Pray for the strength and courage to remain positive. Ask for spiritual support as many times a day as you need.

Thoughts to Think

"I say yes to my ideas. I am willing to begin with what I have. I trust that as I move forward, everything I need will be provided."

THE SPIRITUAL LAW OF PEACE

Peace is with you *always*. You can experience this truth when you aren't struggling to repress your true self.

Peace is constantly flowing within you regardless of your imperfections, weaknesses, and faults. It doesn't stop just because you've made mistakes. Take some time to adjust your mind. Acknowledge that you are worthy of experiencing all the good that life has to offer.

Self-denial causes instability and unrest. When you race away from yourself and refuse to admit that you have shortcomings, you try to create a false sense of liveliness. Regardless of how negative, nasty, or sometimes illegal this masked pleasure is, you know it's not authentic.

Self-acceptance not only soothes your soul, but calms your nerves as well. Yet, you don't want to be yourself if you have faults or weaknesses. As you try to 'freeze time' by dwelling in the past or rush ahead into the future through fantasy, you miss the opportunity to connect with your genuine self. You don't have to *like* everything within yourself, but to transform negativity, you must first accept that it exists.

Whispers of wisdom will fill you as the strength of truth builds you. Let yourself be.

The Spiritual Law of Peace

Summary

Peace is with you always.

Peace is constantly flowing within you regardless of your imperfections, faults, and foibles.

Self-denial causes instability and unrest.

You want to be healed without taking the time to heal yourself.

Self-acceptance allows for genuine connection with others.

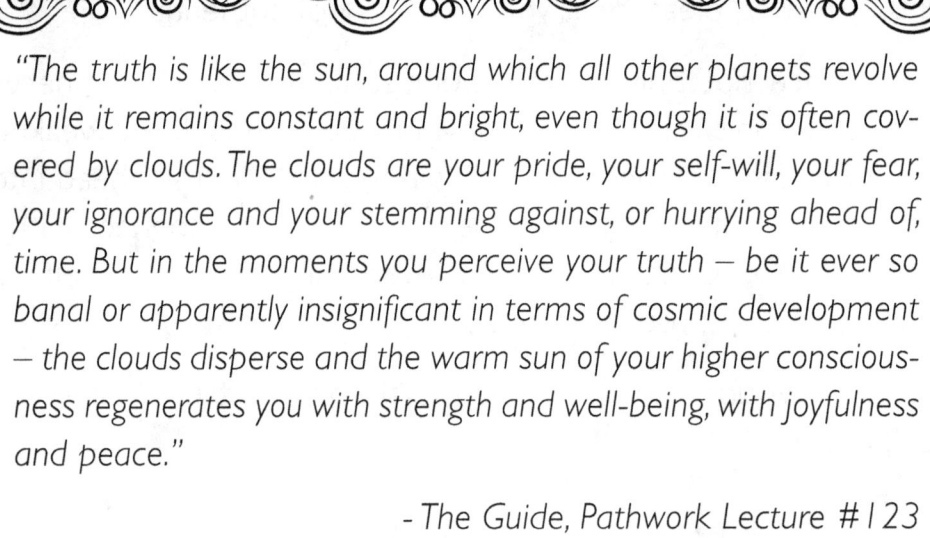

"The truth is like the sun, around which all other planets revolve while it remains constant and bright, even though it is often covered by clouds. The clouds are your pride, your self-will, your fear, your ignorance and your stemming against, or hurrying ahead of, time. But in the moments you perceive your truth — be it ever so banal or apparently insignificant in terms of cosmic development — the clouds disperse and the warm sun of your higher consciousness regenerates you with strength and well-being, with joyfulness and peace."

- The Guide, Pathwork Lecture #123
Liberation and Peace by Overcoming Fear of the Unknown

Realign With Your Spiritual Mind

Spiritual Law: Peace

Violation: Fear

Violating Behaviors: Abandonment of real self, agitation, anxiety, unhappiness, self-pity

Peace Challenge

1. Evaluate your willingness to truly accept yourself as you are. (Use a scale from 1 – 10. 1 = 'not at all'; 10 = 'completely accept myself'.)

2. Is there a direct connection between your self-criticism, harsh judgment and lack of inner peace?

3. How often do you avoid being in the present because your feelings are too uncomfortable? What belief says you're not strong enough to face these feelings?

4. Write down any thoughts and/or beliefs that maintain your uncomfortable feelings. Example: "_____ is making me feel this way." "If _____ wasn't in my life, I could achieve a state of peace."

5. Once you have written your beliefs down on paper, identify which lower self trait(s) is/are causing you lack of inner peace, i.e., blaming another person for your discomfort.

Thoughts to Think

"My true self is peaceful. I accept myself for who I truly am."

THE SPIRITUAL LAW OF PERFECTION

In God's spirit world, everything already exists in perfect order. You can sense this truth when you align with the perfection of your spiritual self; the part of you that remains untouched by human experience.

Your spiritual self contains everything you need to fulfill your life's task. You are meant to function perfectly and deep down you know this. Just think of the high expectations you have of your physical health. When something is wrong, you question, "What's wrong?" or "How can I make myself better?" Yet, you don't hold the same standard to your mental and emotional states. When you feel mentally or emotionally imbalanced, you don't question yourself as quickly. Or, you judge yourself for having critical thoughts and/or negative feelings so you try to ignore or suppress them. All the while you're moving further away from your spiritual mind exposing yourself to more and more anxiety, depression and disharmony. There are even times when you believe that happiness isn't meant for you. But when you align with your spiritual self you are reminded that this isn't true.

The supreme intelligence of your spiritual mind knows which thoughts you should nurture and which ones you should starve. Wisdom feeds you with healthy thoughts of harmony and happiness. Wherever there is disharmony or discomfort, you can be sure that you have moved away from a spiritual truth. Starve the unhealthy inner critic that causes you ill health. Let these thought-forms go unfed.

Spiritual development isn't about becoming perfect. You simply have to remember that you already are.

The Spiritual Law of Perfection

Summary

In God's spirit world, everything already exists in perfect order.

You are meant to function perfectly and deep down you know this.

You criticize yourself for being judgmental or having pain instead of identifying the root cause of its existence.

The supreme intelligence of your spiritual mind knows what thoughts you should nurture and what intentions you should starve.

> *"Your physical system works in absolute perfection when the laws governing it are adhered to. The less you observe them – whether through ignorance or deliberate self-destructiveness – the more you move away from that level on which physical perfection is a reality. By nature, your mental and emotional life is meant to function perfectly, just as your body is. When you achieve this original level, you are home. You have reached that place within yourself that can procure what life is meant to fulfill in you, and what you are meant to fulfill in life – for the two are one."*
>
> *- The Guide, Pathwork Lecture # 141*
> *Return To the Original Level of Perfection*

Realign With Your Spiritual Mind

Spiritual Law: Perfection

Violation: Ignorance

Violating Behaviors: Anguish, confusion, disorder, insecurity, perplexity

Perfection Challenge

1. Think of something you would like to improve about yourself. Then sit in a comfortable position and ask your spiritual self to show you an image of your 'perfect' state. Write down what is presented to you.

2. What do you have to change so you can maintain a steady connection with it?

Thoughts to Think

"My authentic self is naturally constructive and productive. Everything I need to fulfill my life's destiny is within me. I will utilize the power of my spiritual mind to guide my thoughts, words, and actions."

THE SPIRITUAL LAW OF PRAYER

Prayer cleanses your soul and opens you up to the grace, love and wisdom of the eternal life force. It streamlines your thoughts with laser beam focus and precision.

Prayer strengthens your ability to concentrate by formulating well-intentioned thoughts. One clear, precise sentence is all you need to achieve a divine effect. You don't have to repeat yourself, beg, plead, or bargain. Trying to bargain with God comes from a lack of trust. Instead of pleading, take some time to self-soothe. Reassure that insecure part of yourself that you've been heard.

It's OK to pray for yourself. In fact, it's necessary if you want your spiritual self to become a part of your daily living. Praying for yourself may be a new concept to you. You may think it's anti-religious or "selfish". Your current practice may focus solely on reciting formal prayers, even if it means saying them without feeling. Or you may have learned that divine intercession only comes by way of 'good' behavior.

Emotional and spiritual development requires much more than the recitation of religious verses. Think of your prayers as a communication vehicle to link your outer self to the most sacred space within you. Spirituality is a *feeling* experience. If you're not feeling your prayers, you're probably not spiritually praying. Opening the channel to your divine mind is a very personal experience. Spiritual prayers reflect your challenges, triggers, achievements and doubts. Many, if not all, are requests to receive clarity, guidance and wisdom about conflicts and relationships.

If you want to become better, wiser, stronger, healthier, and happier, pray. Ask *sincerely* for God's help. If you are feeling lonely, saddened, powerless, or desolate, pray and ask *whole-heartedly* for guidance. If you are frightened and anxious, *humble* yourself and ask for protection and guidance. Pray to receive only the truth. Pray for the courage to accept the truth. Then pray for your loved ones and your enemies.

If you don't know how to pray, then let the following be your prayer: Humbly ask: "God, please teach me how to pray."

Think of prayer as learning how to speak a new language. Try to stay positive during the learning curve, especially when you don't receive an immediate answer. Divine messages can't always take the fast track. While traveling from the deepest source within, they get quite a lot of push back from defensive, inner resistance.

Angels and spirit guides who are fully equipped, ready to assist, and grateful to fulfill the task of comforting you are always available.

"Knock and it shall be opened unto you."
Matthew 7: 7-8

The Spiritual Law of Prayer

Summary

Prayer cleanses your soul and opens you up to the grace, love, and wisdom of the eternal life force.

Prayer develops focus by formulating well-intentioned thoughts.

It's OK to pray for yourself.

If you're not feeling your prayers, you're probably not spiritually praying.

If you don't know how to pray, humbly ask, "God, please teach me how to pray."

"Prayer is a preliminary step to meditation. Prayer is a matter of thinking, meditation is prayer with feeling, it engages the soul forces as compared to the thinking forces. To get to the second and further step you need a certain discipline and concentration which you learn through prayer. Concentration in prayer is beneficial not only as a training, but also because each thought builds a form. With the thoughts of prayer you build harmonious forms, so that the "thought-prayer" activates favorable energies even before you have learned the "feeling-prayer" or meditation. Yet thought-forms, though they may not have the power of feeling forms, can nevertheless manifest their own greatness when coming from a full heart, without self-deception, rooted in sincere willpower.

- The Guide, Pathwork Lecture # 9
Prayer and Meditation – The Lord's Prayer

Realign With Your Spiritual Mind

Spiritual Law: Prayer

Violation: Resistance

Violating Behaviors: Arrogance, hostility, intolerance, inferiority and superiority complexes

Prayer Challenge

1. Write down one of your prayers. Is your prayer clear and concise? Do you repeat yourself? Clarify what you really want to say or ask, then rewrite your prayer with specificity.

2. Write a prayer that expresses your sincere desire to grow spiritually. Allow your words to express *why* you really want this.

3. Pray for yourself, for others, for peace, and for the spreading of truth throughout the world. If you're uncomfortable praying for someone in particular, be honest and specific about that in your prayer, for example:

   "I am feeling _____ about _____. Although I am praying for peace, I recognize the discordance within myself about _____."

   "I am trying to change my feelings about _____, but I can't (or won't). I ask for clarity to see the greater truth so I can resolve this inner conflict."

Thoughts to Think

"When I pray, my mind shifts and I can feel my authentic self. I pray to be divinely guided in all of my daily affairs."

THE SPIRITUAL LAW OF PRESENCE

Your spiritual self is accessible in present time. As you bring yourself fully present emotionally, mentally and physically, you merge with your God consciousness and you are led by the highest within yourself.

Being present is no small task, but your presence is necessary for spiritual experiences. When your mind is busy rehashing the past or fantasizing about the future, you miss the opportunity to connect with the purest source within yourself. Take a moment to reflect on how often you are truly present. Do you try to escape real time through fantasizing and wishful thinking? Some of these imagined wishes may even come true. If so, will you choose to be present when they manifest?

Presence builds strength. It allows you to objectively confront your misconceptions. You can make new choices when you're present. You can identify negativity that doesn't sustain your spiritual health. Just because you acknowledge 'yukky', self-loathing beliefs doesn't mean you have to hold on to them. You can dissolve any belief that doesn't serve your best self.

You create your thoughts and therefore, you can change them.

The Spiritual Law of Presence
Summary

As you connect with your divinity, you merge with God and you are led by the highest within yourself.

Your presence is necessary for spiritual growth and emotional development.

Just because you acknowledge 'yukky', self-loathing beliefs doesn't mean you have to hold on to them.

Presence allows you to objectively confront your misconceptions.

God meets you in present time.

"To the exact degree self-liking exists, to that degree happiness exists. Lack of self-liking prevents the psyche from experiencing its natural state. It induces an alienation from the universal forces and sets up a screen, or a film preventing the individual from becoming part of the cosmic forces, which <u>are</u> bliss. It does not matter whether the lack of self-liking is based on realistic or unrealistic reasons. Both present an equal obstacle. In the last analysis, it is therefore always a question of a violation of personal integrity which prevents the personality from coming into his own - - whether or not it also causes false guilts."

- The Guide, Pathwork Lecture # 150
Self-liking, Condition for Universal State of Bliss

Realign With Your Spiritual Mind

Spiritual Law: Presence

Violation: Absence; neglect of the real self

Violating Behaviors: Avoidance, fear, frustration, infatuation, resignation, pretension

Presence Challenge

1. Find a comfortable position for self-reflection. State with sincere intention: "I pray for the courage and strength to recognize the misconception(s) that block me from being present." As your mind begins to reveal images and memories, write them down.

2. Observe and evaluate the accuracy of each image, memory and feeling. Acknowledge any resistance you may have toward confronting it.

3. Pray and ask your spiritual self to inspire and fill you with current information that will help you dissolve any destructive thoughts.

Thoughts to Think

"The universe exists and creates in present time. As I choose to be present, I align with eternal, universal presence."

THE SPIRITUAL LAW OF RELAXATION

Relaxation is a dynamic movement that is alive, yet calming. The relaxed state is a peaceful energetic force that is fueled by a happy-go-lucky and light-hearted attitude.

You have everything you need to feel calm throughout your day. You may know this intellectually, but still find yourself struggling to relax. If so, check in and see if you're trying to rationalize your emotions away.

Intensity and other aggressive behaviors can often be misconstrued as passionate involvement. Light-heartedness can be mistakenly perceived as weak or not caring enough. These misconceptions couldn't be further from the truth. Stressful, intense thoughts cause a rigid inner constriction that prevents life force from flowing freely.

Try to objectively observe your self-talk. Are you kind to yourself? Or do you make cruel statements such as: 'I should know this already!', 'I'm not capable enough!' 'I'll never be chosen!'? If so, change it. For example, when feeling pressured, you can say something to yourself like, 'Instead of feeling overwhelmed, I'll ask for help, or more time, or more information, or whatever, *so I can get what I need.*' As you fulfill your needs, you will feel more fulfilled, *less anxious,* and more relaxed.

Kindness, consideration, and self-care always create a relaxed state of mind. Learn how to identify when your intensity is masking your fear. Learn to recognize when strict seriousness pretends to be your helpful friend. For as long as fear dictates, you will remain inflexible.

The Spiritual Law of Relaxation

Summary

Relaxation is a dynamic movement that is alive, yet calming.

The relaxed state is a powerful, energetic force that is fueled by a happy-go-lucky and light-hearted attitude.

Intensity and other aggressive behaviors are often mistaken for being passionately engaged or meaningfully involved.

Intensity, rigidity, and stress are not something that can be intellectualized away; confront them head-on to identify their root cause.

"People's habitual state is one of more or less taut intensity which is foreign to and incompatible with the universal power. In order to be compatible with the universal power, it is necessary that the personality is in inner and outer relaxation. Such relaxation does not imply immobility, nor lack of energy. It is not the kind of false relaxation that does not breathe, move, or respond. Quite the contrary. It expands and contracts like breathing — is rhythmic and relaxed; effortless, yet vibrating with power, poised and calm, peaceful and dynamic. This state, when attempting to describe it, may easily be confused with indifference, passivity, or laxness. It is none of these. But it is entirely free from tension due to fear, pride, and self will."

- The Guide, Pathwork Lecture #151
Intensity: An Obstacle to Self-Realization

Realign With Your Spiritual Mind

Spiritual Law: Relaxation

Violation: Intensity

Violating Behaviors: Dramatization, Inflexibility, Rigidity, Stress, Severity, Stagnation

Relaxation Challenge

1. Observe where your physical body may be tense or constricted. Dialogue with it, ask: "Why are you so tight?" Listen and try to identify the belief that is holding the tension.

2. How often do you respond with habitual behavior because you won't acknowledge your real feelings? What feelings are you avoiding?

3. Allow your real feelings to surface. Are you still reluctant to acknowledge something about yourself? If so, why?

Thoughts to Think

"My natural state is relaxed and calm. I will lean into any tension that exists within my mind and body until it melts so life force can flow effortlessly.

THE SPIRITUAL LAW OF RESPONSIBILITY

Responsible ideas create powerful thought-forms that draw divine substance from and to you. Jesus Christ, Mahatma Ghandi, The Dali Lama, Buddha, and many other spiritual masters have relied upon this powerful force to fulfill their life's tasks.

The power of your internal life force becomes immediately available to you through acts of responsibility. The more reliable you are, the more strength you have to carry out your tasks. Responsibility activates and increases positive energy flow that allows you to give so much more of yourself. Old, destructive psychic structures lose their momentum and start to fade away. Weaknesses dissolve and you are filled with the strength and energy of integrity and truth.

Accountability, courage, patience, and loving kindness are responsible behaviors that connect you with your inner divinity. Traits that nourish and fortify spiritual muscle.

The Spiritual Law of Responsibility

Summary

Accountability, courage, patience and loving kindness are responsible behaviors that connect you with your divinity.

You activate internal life force when you act responsibly.

Responsible ideas create powerful thought-forms that draw more divine substance from and to you.

> *"Creative substance is the most powerful energy. It is the most fertile life stuff imaginable. Its malleability, its responsiveness to creating mind, is as infinite as the universe itself. Whatever consciousness can conceive of and express in thought, feeling, and will-direction, creative life substance molds, forms, builds. To know and experience this is to be connected with the process of creation, a process which is ongoing and available to all living creatures. To know this is key to the human struggle. If you can assume responsibility for the undesirable occurrences in your life, no matter what they may be, by establishing your own resistance to expansion, you have made a major step toward the removal of your blocks."*
>
> *- The Guide, Pathwork Lecture # 181*
> *The Meaning of The Human Struggle*

Realign With Your Spiritual Mind

Spiritual Law: Responsibility

Violation: Irresponsibility

Violating Behaviors: Carelessness, inconsideration, laziness, recklessness, unaccountability

Self-Responsibility Challenge

1. Identify a situation that turned out satisfactorily because you took responsibility.

2. What behaviors did you demonstrate that attributed to your success?

3. Pray and ask for guidance on how to become more responsible where you are still acting irresponsibly. Visualize a positive outcome and write down the responsible behaviors that would be necessary to achieve it.

Thoughts to Think

"I have everything within me to live a productive and constructive life. I commit to being a responsible person and refuse to blame anyone for my circumstances."

THE SPIRITUAL LAW OF SURRENDER

From the depths of the surrendered soul, divine creations stream forth effortlessly. Meaningful poetry, rhythmic dance and beautiful music are nothing short of God's creative expression. We are surrounded by multiple signs of divine beauty and intelligence. Yet surrendering to this most dynamic pulse of which we are all a part, requires courage.

When you surrender, you may experience doubt or a sense of emptiness. You may feel nothing at all. Or, you may have to confront parts of yourself that you've intentionally buried for years. Self-imposed, restricted areas that you designated as 'unsafe' so you wouldn't have to face the hatred, jealousy, or resentment that you consider too painful to acknowledge. But how will you merge with your spiritual self if these barriers remain in your way?

Trust.

Trust and faith. Think of all the people to whom you've entrusted your darkest secrets. Your spouse, coach, teacher, minister, parent or anyone else that you openly share yourself with requires the act of surrender. Humbling yourself to surrender also assists in breaking down unnecessary defense mechanisms.

The act of surrendering also builds faith. When you let go, you experience a connection to your true self. You can 'hear' the voice of your inner knowing as it guides your emotions. You learn to count on this presence within you. You know there's something greater in charge because you're now one with it.

Your spiritual mind will guide you where your outer intellect never will. Take a knee to your spiritual vow.

The Spiritual Law of Surrender

Summary

When you surrender, you may experience doubt or a sense of emptiness.

Trust.

Surrender builds faith.

Letting go creates a deep connection to your true self.

> *"A human being who is incapable of surrendering cannot find his core. He cannot find his divine nature. He cannot love. He cannot truly learn and grow. Such an individual is a very stiff, defended and closed up structure. The ability to surrender is an essential inner movement from which all that is good can flow. You need to surrender to the will of God. Otherwise you will always remain attached to the very shortsighted and the much pain- and confusion- producing self-will. Surrender means a letting go of self, of cherished ideas, goals, desires, opinions -- all for the sake of truth. For God is truth."*
>
> *- The Guide, Pathwork Lecture # 254*
> *Surrender*

Realign With Your Spiritual Mind

Spiritual Law: Surrender

Violation: Rigidity

Violating Behaviors: Arrogance, cowardice, distrust, suspicion, stubbornness

Surrender Challenge

1. What is your definition of surrender?

2. Write down all of your reactions when you think of surrendering to your inner divinity.

3. Create a daily plan that allows you to make contact with your spiritual self, (i.e., 15 minute meditation, daily review, etc.)

Thoughts to Think

"I choose to surrender and align with my spiritual power."

THE SPIRITUAL LAW OF TRUTH

Where there is truth, there is love. Where there is love, there is God. Where there is not love, spiritual awareness is lacking.

The search for truth is the ultimate quest in getting to know your real self. Truth creates an open, uninhibited state in your emotional body that generates the strength and courage to feel anything. If you're unsure about what the truth is, you can 'check-in'. Your body and feelings will let you know.

Truth emits calm and has a calming effect, even when you're facing something that's really painful. Genuine sadness will travel smoothly through your system without getting stuck in defended states of fear. Truth provides the solid, inner foundation that allows your feelings to flow and exit the body.

Fear instills feelings of anxiety, doubt, confusion, worry, and all other defensive, negative expressions. Anxiety is an emotional reaction to something you fear. When you're feeling anxious – pause for a moment and ask yourself, "What am I afraid of?" You can decrease anxiety by addressing it head-on. You can tune into the specific thought-forms that frighten you. Once you are aware of your misconceptions, you can re-educate yourself with the truth.

Re-educating fear-based thoughts is an essential step in emotional and spiritual transformation. Emotional development is the most challenging phase of spiritual growth as many thoughts are unconscious. A devoted practice of self-awareness will enlighten your mind and free your soul.

The Spiritual Law of Truth

Summary

Where there is love, there is truth. Where there is truth, there is God.

Where there is not love, spiritual awareness is lacking.

Anxiety is an emotional reaction to fear.

Re-educating fearful thoughts is key to emotional and spiritual development.

> *"…when you are in doubt you are depressed, and when you are experiencing truth, you feel happy. Truth must always make you happy – even unpleasant truth. All my friends on the path have experienced how they must occasionally encounter unflattering or unpleasant aspects of themselves. But when desire for the truth within becomes greater than all else, this unpleasant truth will always strengthen and bring happiness. By the same token, if you observe your feelings closely, you will find that untruth, pleasant as it may seem at the moment, never gives you real peace, for deep down your higher self always has the correct answer and you must feel it. This truth will never depress you."*
>
> *- The Guide, Pathwork Lecture # 13*
> *Positive Thinking: The Right and the Wrong Kind*

Realign With Your Spiritual Mind

Law: Truth

Violation: Ignorance

Violating Behaviors: Cheating, deception, denial, lying, manipulation, omission

Truth Challenge

1. Think of a personal or professional relationship that is causing you distress. Imagine yourself sitting down with this person.

2. As you visualize yourself talking to this person, allow yourself to feel and express all of your emotions.

3. After you've released your emotions, reflect. Pause long enough to identify the error(s) and distortion(s) in your thinking that contribute to your troubled emotion(s).

Thoughts to Think

"I am willing to let go of my vanity, pride, and self-will to experience the power of truth."

THE SPIRITUAL LAW OF UNITY

Your spirit is *always* with you. It remains intact during the entirety of your life-time. When you set your intention to align with your spiritual self, you create the proper inner conditions to access divine intelligence. Spiritual inspiration is revealed to you in ways you can personally understand.

> *"The disparate elements I'd begun with ten years before had become unified; my road experience had made me tough as steel, and I had total command of my material. But most important, I felt really, really funny."*
>
> Steve Martin, Comedian, Author, 'Born Standing Up'

Great Book. Read it if you want a real life example of achieving the unified state.

Emotional beliefs are birthed in human experience and shouldn't be confused with eternal truth. When you are open enough and ready to give up limited, dualistic thinking for the sake of truth, your spiritual self will emerge.

Your divine intelligence is inclusive. It provides insight into other's perspectives and opinions. Its depth of understanding always offers comfort. This profound connection that runs through you has lasting value. Dualistic thoughts such as either/or, good/bad, and right/wrong finally lose their power. A sense of completeness fills you as your spiritual values integrate with your human behaviors.

Union with God happens when you give up dualistic thinking for the sake of truth.

The Spiritual Law of Unity

Summary

Your spirit is always available to you.

Emotional beliefs are birthed in human experience and shouldn't be confused with eternal truth.

Your divine intelligence is inclusive.

Union with God happens when you give up dualistic thinking for the sake of truth.

> *"On the unified plane of consciousness there are no opposites. There is no good or bad, no right or wrong, no life or death. There is only good, only right, only life. The unified state of consciousness is attained through understanding or knowingness. You already have, in your real self, a unified state of mind, regardless of how unconscious and ignorant you may be of it ... Now, even those who have never heard of such a thing have a deep longing and a mostly unconscious sense of a different state of mind and life experience than the one they know. They yearn for the freedom, blissfulness, and mastery of life that the unified state of consciousness affords."*
>
> *- The Guide, Pathwork Lecture # 143*
> *Unity and Duality*

Realign With Your Spiritual Mind

Spiritual Law: Unity

Violation: Separation

Violating Behaviors: Antagonism, disharmony, inferiority, isolation, narcissism

Unity Challenge

1. Think of a person that triggers discomfort or negativity within you. Write down all the things you don't like about this person.

2. Next, imagine yourself in this person's shoes. From this person's perspective, write down all the things that they *may* think of you.

3. Meditate and ask to be open to receive a unified perspective about this matter. Pray for the courage to accept the truth, even if it's not what you want to acknowledge. Pray for the strength to dissolve any resistance you may have. Write down what comes to you.

Thoughts to Think

"I am willing to accept the truth and receive a unified perspective that centers me in calm."

*It is only when we get in touch with our innate,
natural rhythm can we feel connected to
what we are doing, to our place in the world, to God.*

PART THREE
WHEN WILL I BEGIN TO FEEL MY SPIRITUAL SELF?

THE SLOW AND STEADY PROCESS OF SPIRITUAL DEVELOPMENT

It takes courage to walk a spiritual path. Connecting with your spiritual self is not an easy task. Tapping into this most sacred part of yourself often requires meeting many misconceptions along the way. You may come across unknown psychic territory that you don't understand. You will undoubtedly find yourself dissolving yet another layer of some ungodly belief that surfaces in your discovery process. It can take days, weeks or months before a unified sense of wholeness becomes your waking reality. No one can really give you a specific date because the unified state isn't something you can buy and suddenly own. The sacred process of spiritual integration happens on its own time.

The defensive attitude "I already know this" is one of the most common deterrents to spiritual growth. This all-knowing 'lower' character trait uses the "been there, done that" attitude to escape the necessary effort and work it takes to evolve. Spiritual development isn't possible when you believe you already know everything. The "done this already" attitude comes from a prideful attitude that tries to convince you that you're already somewhere that you're not, yet.

Instead of giving into the 'know-it-all' attitude, try a different approach by praying, "I already reviewed this, but I am committed to my spiritual path. I want to explore myself with a fresh perspective." You can also ask for spiritual strength to grow. You can pray, "Please grant me the strength and courage to see all aspects of myself as I am. I wish to restore truth where there is still distortion within my mind." This genuine approach will attract the corresponding healing energies from God's spirit world.

All human behavior that deviates from the spiritual self can be narrowed down to the following three human faults:

Self-Will: Wanting something for yourself that is not aligned with God's will. Selfish motivations driven by self-interest, force and/or manipulation when others are unwilling to 'go along'.

Pride: A false, inflated or deflated self-image that causes strong negative emotional reactions such as disappointment, rage, etc. when expectations aren't met. Images of pride range from very poor ideas about the self to grandiose and narcissistic.

Fear: The mental, emotional and/or physical response you experience when you're not aligned in truth.

Psychotherapy, behavioral redirection and wellness techniques such as yoga, guided imagery, and mindfulness are very helpful tools to cultivate balance and calm, but they are not enough when you aspire to evolve spiritually. Spiritual development requires consistent, daily prayer and meditation, self-honesty, and a humble attitude to align with your spiritual self.

PRAYER – PATHWAY TO YOUR SPIRITUAL SELF

Prayer builds a solid, steady bridge from your conscious mind to your spiritual self. When the counsel of God's spirit world is genuinely sought, an answer from that sphere of consciousness is provided.

Accessing your spiritual power and strength through prayer isn't just for the sake of removing an annoying symptom, although it can and will do that. The purpose of accessing your spiritual self is to make it readily available so you can experience the scintillating life force that is very much alive and real within you. Your spiritual mind can invoke revitalization on all levels. Your feelings become rejuvenated and your perception is accurate. Beliefs that are not aligned in truth peel away, making room for more vibrant, genuine experiences.

Continue to ask God for clarity when you're unclear about an answer. The answers will come as you dig deeper and remain consistent in your willingness to know more. Stay connected through sincere, humble intentions. Ask again and again *without begging*. If you need a role model, think of your favorite journalist who's uncovered a great story. Any successful journalist continues to ask questions until all the facts are gathered. To get to the root, the real fruit of the story, persistence is necessary. Asking in prayer is similar. A consistent, yet relaxed routine practice of prayer strengthens your ability to access universal truths. Over time, you strengthen your spiritual alignment and make yourself ready to receive the eternal truths. You must not give up.

Don't be too quick to dismiss internal messages. If you don't understand an inner image that appears in your mind's eye, or a feeling or memory that surfaces, remain present and ask for clarity. If you ignore your inner communications, you may be throwing away very valuable information.

If you don't know how or have forgotten how to pray, you can refer to the Spiritual Law of Prayer in Part Two: Spiritual Laws to Access Your Divine Self.

Spiritual Healing

A spiritual healing occurs when the eternal life force transforms a mental, emotional or physical impurity. Ever so subtly, spiritual healing energy can penetrate the mental and emotional levels without a hint of physical evidence. Small changes in attitudes, beliefs, and opinions can manifest daily without the effects reaching the outer personality for quite some time. Most spiritual healings happen this way, but to the eye of an ignorant observer, it never occured. "If it's not healed physically, then it's not healed" is often said by the same people who don't acknowledge the existence of inner life. It's unfortunate that the outer mind has a tendency to predispose and judge so quickly.

Spiritual Warfare

You may at times feel overwhelmed by strong negative emotions that seem to come out of nowhere. They may even take you by surprise. It may be more surprising to learn that *all* negativity stems from self-loathing, low self-esteem and lack of self-love. I know, hard to believe at first especially when nasty situations that justify your feelings are staring you in the face. But if you remain open enough and want to purify your soul and view your negative reactions as opportunity for growth, you will be shown this truth.

If someone around you is acting out negatively, their thought and intention is negative too. They may not be *consciously* aware of their negative intention, but it's deliberate nonetheless. However unpleasant this may be, it can actually be a valuable experience for you to spend time with this person. You will have to decide. There are times when you can fulfill a spiritual task that supports your own development while trying to help another. Shining light, conveying a truth, or providing a neutral, objective viewpoint can dissipate emotional toxicity. Or, it may be that you are supposed to stay away from such negativity. A person could be at such a low level of development that it would be dangerous for you to be around them. When you're open and willing enough to receive the intelligence of your spiritual mind, you will receive divine guidance and know what is right for you.

Another common battle of spiritual warfare is when a person with low, negative frequencies is in the presence of a person who emanates much light. The brightness of the more evolved person is actually painful for the negative person. Imagine yourself walking out into a bright, sunny parking lot after sitting in a dark movie theater for two hours. Your immediate reaction would be to squint and shield your eyes from the light. A person who is wedded to their negativity has a similar response. If the surrounding personalities are too bright, the person hosting the negativity can't survive. They will cringe, complain, or try to dominate with ugly maneuvers. When their attempts prove unsuccessful, they will inevitably disappear.

However uncomfortable the light may be for the person who wants to transform, it's best to grin and bear it. The light and people who emanate it can help dissuade and eventually dissolve such negative forces.

*A psychological issue can never be completely
healed until it is addressed as a spiritual issue.*

Visualization – A Deeply Profound Spiritual Practice

Visualizing your future self is a powerful tool for spiritual growth. The following is an example of what life looks like when your spiritual self is involved:

Your life is full because you know you are worthy of abundance. You accept that you are part of the divine, so you willingly consult your spiritual mind. You balance your day by meeting and greeting your inner divinity. You allow for the grace of Its presence to fill you with your daily dose of wisdom. You engage confidently in your relationships knowing that your spiritual self considers the best for all of you. You look forward to freely sharing your true self with others. You are relaxed and create joyously, knowing that you are growing in your individuality. The purity of your presence attracts opportunities that fulfill, enlighten, and empower you, and all those who surround you.

The validity of your visualizations can be assessed by the satisfaction and fulfillment of your outer life. How satisfied are you? Are you living your cherished desires? Are you happy? If not, practice visualizing what you deeply long for. See yourself living an abundant and fulfilling life. Practice the visualization process daily.

Recognizing Yourself in Others

Exemplary role models are all around you. So are others who are less ideal. If you are happy with your direction in life, continue to expand your happiness. If you are unfulfilled, plant new seeds in your mind. Pray for direction and guidance to discover the root cause of your dissatisfaction. Meanwhile, as you wait for your new ideas to sprout, work to dissolve the inner images that prevent you from achieving your desires. Also work to identify the parent figure that you're unconsciously 'mirroring'. Just because they're your parents doesn't mean you have to mimic them.

The Atomic Now

Science has already discovered the power of the atom. Something so small it can't be detected by the physical eye, yet a force so powerful it can obliterate millions of people and wipe out entire cities. This fact certainly changes the idea that what is larger is more powerful.

The power of the atom is a spiritual force that is also available to you. It is your birthright to experience the power of your spirit anytime you wish. Regardless of any emotional, mental or physical imbalances you may experience, you can access this eternal force – *at any time*. Your human imperfections don't have to be completely cleared. Perfection is not necessary to experience another part of yourself. Think about it. If you're allowed to feel sadness, happiness, strength, or weakness, why would you be denied to feel the best and most powerful part of yourself?

EXERCISE

The Atomic Now Challenge:

Do you want to give up caffeine or sugar, but don't have an alternative to give you a similar boost? If you're willing to *fully* surrender to your spiritual power, you can experience it, regardless of anything and everything that's happening around you. Allow yourself to melt into the core of your being where the calm, rhythmic pattern of the eternal now pulsates within you. Give yourself permission to rise to your inner bliss. Set a positive, constructive intention to merge with your divinity, your true self.

Through practice and over time, your spiritual mind becomes more accessible. If you persist in your spiritual practice, you will no longer need or want coffee, sugar, or anything else that is supposed to substitute what your soul knows can never be replaced.

AM I GETTING ANYWHERE?

The question "How am I doing?" will eventually come up while pursuing a quest of spiritual awakening. You'll want to know how far you've come. You'll want to know where this is going. You'll want to know why you can't seem to maintain a *continual* connection to your spiritual self. You'll ask questions like, "Why is it so hard to stop my negative thoughts?" "How can I tell if my thoughts are fear-based and not grounded in reality?" "How long will it take for me to recognize thoughts from my spiritual self?"

I usually respond to these types of questions with a question of my own, "Which level of your consciousness is asking?"

Your spirit knows when you've left it behind. From infancy, you were taught to look outwardly for answers, strength, guidance, and fulfillment. Therapists, clergy members, spouses, teachers and good friends have become your truth surrogates, often leaving the river of spiritual intelligence untapped.

Spiritual growth is an on-going, ever-evolving process. You can vacillate back and forth between several states of consciousness, including your spiritual self, within the course of a year, month, day, or even an hour. Self-awareness and a commitment to spiritual purification are the keys to success in personal enlightenment. Not time.

But even those who walk a spiritual path with great devotion still have blind spots. There are many people who are already committed to the *behaviors* of a spiritual life. They want to be better spouses, parents, siblings, employers, employees and better, caring children to their aging parents. And most already are. But spiritual force isn't activated by acting 'good'.

The sole purpose of your spiritual self is to guide you in your unification process. In the final analysis, God never says no. Whenever you experience anything less than happiness and fulfillment, consider it divine notice. It's a reminder that you've left your spiritual self behind. It's a call back to the internal, universal force of which you are an important part.

PART FOUR
THE SPIRITUAL MIND IN DREAMS

THE IMPORTANCE OF DREAMS

Dreams are continuously sending brilliant tips, guidance and advice. The language of dreams is very similar to spiritual language. Dream messages are primarily communicated through images, pictures and symbols. The messages of your unconscious mind invariably represent your personal beliefs, opinions, attitudes, and feelings. Sometimes very strong feelings.

In dreams, colors will often be important clues that represent emotion. For example, shadowy grays and muddy browns often reflect dark, heavy emotions. Yellows, pinks, and other soft hues represent brilliant, higher states of consciousness.

You can learn how to interpret the valuable messages of your dreams through a systematic approach of dream interpretation. Use the worksheets provided at the end of this section and you will be well on your way to understanding the voice of your unconscious mind. If you have trouble remembering your dreams, go to the 'Tips on How to Remember Your Dreams' worksheet to help you remember them.

The Most Famous Dream of All

Understanding the language of dreams can be tricky at first. To effectively demonstrate how dream images communicate, I have chosen Dorothy's dream from the movie, 'The Wizard of Oz'. To refresh your memory, a brief synopsis of the movie is summarized below:

The story opens at a little farm in Kansas where Dorothy and her dog Toto live with her Auntie Em and Uncle Henry. A wickedly cruel neighbor, Mrs. Gulch, tries to take Dorothy's dog Toto away because he gets into her garden. Dorothy complains to her Auntie Em and Uncle Henry, but they're too busy to listen. Dorothy turns to the three farmhands, Zeke, Hunk, and Hickory for advice. Hunk tells Dorothy that she has to use her brains and stand up to Mrs. Gulch. "Your head isn't made of straw, you know." Zeke advises, "Have a little courage. Spit in her eye." When Hickory tries to chime in, he's rudely interrupted by Auntie Em: "Get your work done or you'll have none." Frozen by her abrupt dismissal and rejection, Hickory doesn't finish his sentence and sadly returns to his farm chores.

Dismayed and bewildered, Dorothy daydreams that *"somewhere out there, high up in the sky, over the rainbow, dreams really do come true"*.

Shortly thereafter, Mrs. Gulch appears with an order from the Sheriff's office. "I'm taking Toto to make sure he's destroyed." Mrs. Gulch grabs Toto and stuffs him into her bicycle basket, but Toto escapes and runs back home to Dorothy.

Dorothy runs away with Toto and meets a charlatan who promotes himself as a 'seer'. He tells Dorothy that someone close to her is very sick and worried. Dorothy knows it is Auntie Em and runs home.

Dorothy struggles as she's confronted by the strong winds of an oncoming twister. She and Toto make it into the farmhouse, but the dangerous winds blow out her bedroom window and knock Dorothy unconscious.

Dorothy's Dream

Dorothy descends into the depths of her unconscious mind where her beliefs, strengths and weaknesses are portrayed in the following dream images: Glinda, the Good Witch of the North; the Wicked Witch of the

West; the Lion; Tinman; Scarecrow; Toto; and the great Wizard of Oz. There are many other colorful and wonderful dream images like flying monkeys and multi-colored horses and munchkins, but in this interpretation I will stick with the main characters only.

Dream Characters

Images	*Meaning*
Glinda, the Good Witch of the North	Spiritual self: wise, calm, voice of reason, inspirational, supportive, and a loving guide.
Toto	Unconditional love
Wicked Witch of the West	Lower traits: greedy, mean, cruel, selfish, self-centered
Lion (Beginning of movie)	Mask: bully, mean, aggressive; then fearful and cowardly when confronted by Dorothy.
Lion (End of movie)	Unmasked – humble, grateful, courageous and kind.
Tinman (Beginning of movie)	Rigid; frozen stiff by rejection
Tinman (End of movie)	Willing to feel; allows his feelings of love and concern to flow freely for Dorothy

Scarecrow (Beginning of movie)	Insecure, self-doubting, timid, fearful, low self-esteem
Scarecrow (End of movie)	Confident, self-assured, poised, assertive, undefended
Wizard of Oz	Inner wisdom – advises all parts of self, (Lion, Tinman, and Scarecrow) to confront fear, "Go and bring me the broom."
Ruby Slippers	Dorothy's spiritual self: *"There's no place like home."*

Summary

Dorothy's Inner and Outer Dilemma Solved

Dorothy must call upon her reasoning faculties (the Scarecrow – i.e., Hunk) to confront her fear (the Wicked Witch – i.e., Mrs. Gulch). Dorothy develops her courage (the Lion – i.e., Zeke) to conquer it. When Dorothy is kidnapped by the Wicked Witch, her friends are so full of love and concern (the Tinman – i.e., HickoryZ) they're willing to do anything to save her. All for the sake of love (Dorothy). Directed by her spiritual mind (Glinda the good witch and the Wizard of Oz), Dorothy knows what to do. At the end of the movie, she learns that she doesn't have to go very far at all to get whatever she needs. That if it's not in her own backyard (the ruby slippers – Dorothy's spiritual self), it's not anywhere.

Dorothy's Inner Growth

Each dream character represents a part of Dorothy that's in need of growth and development. Throughout the story, each character takes the necessary steps to grow and by the end Dorothy stands secure, complete and 'at home' within herself.

> *Understanding your inner imagery brings you a step closer*
> *to spiritual reality, the existence behind physical matter.*

ACKNOWLEDGING YOUR SPIRITUAL MIND IN DREAMS

If you are having difficulty connecting with your spiritual self, you can safely assume that an unconscious 'no' is blocking your way. The following dream brings light to a hidden, unconscious 'no'.

For confidentiality purposes, the client and her family members' names have been changed.

During the phone session described below, Sharon expressed that although the 'new age' therapy she received in the past helped her self-esteem, it included a lot of focus on universal energy, oneness, and "blah, blah, blah", but it really didn't help much in developing a faith in God.

The following case study focuses on Sharon's dream revealing a deeply embedded, negative intention.

Background: Sharon has one son, Mark, who is married and has three children. Mark and his wife are devout Christians who have a very strong faith and personal relationship with Christ. Sharon considers herself to be very close with Mark and his family. They have shared many conversations about their differing beliefs in God and Jesus Christ.

Note: In her waking life, Sharon recently became aware of a misconception that had been ruling her life: "Mom's always right. I'm always wrong."

Sharon's Dream

Mark (Sharon's son) was getting married to a man who was toned and physically fit, but had an old, pasty white face and wore glasses. In the dream, Sharon was horrified and screaming "NO!" Sharon woke up and was disturbed by her dream throughout the day.

I began the dream interpretation by asking the following:

K: What does Mark represent to you?

S: I immediately think of Christ. And the bible; Mark is so dedicated to scripture. My God. He loves God.

K: Does the pasty white face guy represent anyone who is currently in your life?

S: I didn't know him in the dream. It was weird. Mark is soooo Christian. It's something he would never do. I mean, marrying a man is against his faith.

K: What do you think of now when you visualize this pasty white face guy?

S: Well, just thinking about him, I want to laugh. He was meek, and kind of scrawny, but he was really, really fit. You know, six-pack kind of abs. That sort of muscular. I don't know how to communicate how odd it was that my son Mark would marry a man. In real life, I mean my waking life, I'm going to a gay marriage ceremony this weekend. So it's not my own prejudice.

K: I don't want to focus on the marriage right now. Are you willing to do an exercise with the dream character?

S: Yes.

K: OK, allow yourself to get settled into a comfortable position and close your eyes.

S: OK, I'm there.

K: Imagine the pasty white face guy in your mind's eye. Give yourself inner space to become him. Lend him your voice box and allow him to communicate why he's in your dream. For instance, "I'm a pasty white face guy. I'm in your dream because…." Let him talk and finish the sentence.

(Sharon became silent. Long pause.)

S: Kathleen, oh Kathleen … I don't know how to say this. It's very humbling.

K: Did he say something?

S: No. No. It isn't words. I was thinking about apologizing to him because I just realized how much I'm mocking and rejecting him. Just how my mother treats me, I'm embarrassed to say. But he gently and caringly doesn't seem to mind. He's there no matter what. Whether I say yes or no. He's a very gentle and humble presence. (Another long, silent pause.) He's going to accept me no matter what. It's very touching….

K: He's there for you.

S: No matter what. It's me, Kathleen. It's me. I'm the one who is saying no to him.

K: And your son Mark? What is Mark doing?

S: He's marrying this ... Well, this presence. He's committing to this beautiful, humbling presence that I'm saying no to.

K: And does this represent anything in your waking life?

S: My no to God. How I say no to anyone who is loving, gentle, or kind. I don't know it in my life. My father was either drunk, or sober and quiet. My mother was very controlling. So now, I say no, but I want to say yes to this.

K: I'm thinking of the God-image. Could it be that what you think God is, isn't that at all?

S: I know deep down that everything is going to be OK, that the other shoe isn't going to drop. But then out of habit, or just to be negative, I'll go into worrying or doubt. I know it's not right, yet I do it anyway.

K: It's courageous to admit your negative intention to remain stuck in your past. It frees you up to make another choice.

S: There's not a whole lot more that I can say. This feels very empowering.

K: Becoming consciously aware of where you say 'no' to God is empowering.

Summary

Sharon's concept of 'God' continues to shift. Her relationship with her mother is becoming more tenable as well. Sharon has begun to separate herself from people in social circles who've been critical and unkind toward her. She now recognizes that rejecting gentleness and kindness from others is a projection of her inner rejection toward 'God'.

To understand the messages from your internal images, become them. Lend your voice box so the images can speak through you.

Tips for Dream Interpretation and Analysis

- The people, places, and things dreamt of represent aspects of your self.

- Feelings in dreams are as important as the symbols.

- Make personal associations with dream characters, objects, and symbols.

- Give 'voice' to your dream characters. In your waking state, become the characters – allow them to speak aloud and voice their thoughts and opinions.

How to Remember Your Dreams

- Ask your unconscious mind to help you remember your dreams before going to sleep – *with genuine sincerity* (The supreme intelligence of the unconscious mind can't be fooled. If you ask half-heartedly, it intuits your insincerity.).

- Keep a pen, notepad, and nightlight by your bed.

- Write down your dreams as soon as you remember them.

- Become friends with your dream characters.

DREAM WORKSHEETS

How to Interpret a Dream

Dream Recall

Below is a list of questions that will help you determine the meaning of a dream. Try and think of your dreams as vignettes, or plays that are conveying a message or theme.

1. What was the theme of your dream?

   _____
   _____

2. Where did your dream take place? Try to recall as many details as possible.

   _____
   _____

3. Who was in your dream? Write down everyone, even if you don't know who they are in your waking life.

   _____
   _____

4. Describe the emotional feelings associated with your dream.

   _____
   _____

Tips for Interviewing Dream Characters

Become the characters and symbols in your dream. Allow them to vocalize their perspective on a particular situation. Listen to the character's thoughts and feelings, regardless of how irrational they may first seem. This is an important step before redirecting behavior toward positive outcomes.

1. Before you begin the dream interview, identify the specific image, symbol, or person that you would like to learn more about. If there are several, then interview all of them.

2. Accept the answer, even if it doesn't make sense at first. Don't analyze or 'edit' responses. This is an intuitive exercise.

3. Answers to dream questions will often lead you in a direction that is unfamiliar to your conscious mind. Just go with the flow and trust it.

4. If you begin to feel anxious or uncomfortable, don't push it. Simply pause and when ready, ask again. Exploring feelings or situations, especially for the first time, can be uncomfortable so be patient with yourself.

5. Have fun and keep the mood lighthearted and playful. Think of this exercise as acting in a play. If something fearful or upsetting comes up, make a note and move on. Enjoy switching roles if you're working with a partner.

Dream Interviews

Imagine yourself as a journalist conducting an interview with your dream images and characters. Try to gather as much information as possible. After you ask each question below, pause to lend your voice box to each dream character or symbol. Allow them to use your voice to answer each question. You can make up questions of your own. Remember, the more questions you ask, the more information you will have to form an accurate and complete story.

Below are some sample interview questions you can ask the dream symbols and characters (Fill in the blank space with the dreamer's name.).

1. Why have you appeared in _____'s dream?

2. Who are you and what do you represent in _____'s life?

3. What message would you like to give _____?

4. Is there anything specific you would like _____ to know about you?

5. What kind of feelings do you provoke in _____?

6. What do you want _____ to know when she feels these feelings?

7. What can _____ learn from your presence in her dream?

Nightmares

One of the best ways to conquer your fears is to review, decipher, and understand the root cause of your feelings in the bad dream.

1. Write down your nightmare and include as many details as possible.
   _____
   _____

2. Describe the images, objects, and people and what was so frightening/disturbing about them. (If animals or other 'beings' were in the dream, write them down too.)
   _____
   _____

3. Was the reaction you had to the threat or attack in your dream similar to any situation you can recall in real life?
   _____
   _____

4. Rewrite the ending of your dream so it has a positive outcome.
   _____
   _____

Dream Dictionary

The language of your unconscious mind will speak to you through symbols that are personal and familiar to you. It's important to make personal associations with images to accurately interpret its meaning. Below is a list of common, everyday words. As practice, write down what immediately comes to your mind after you read each word. Don't give it too much thought. This is an exercise in the process of 'free association'.

Airplane _____   Monster _____

Automobile _____   Pumpkin _____

Ball _____   Purse _____

Basement _____   Raccoon _____

Beach _____   Roses _____

Classroom _____   Snake _____

Flowers _____   Swimming _____

Green _____   Sun _____

Hat _____   Water _____

Knife _____   Zoo _____

PART FIVE
CASE STUDIES AND ADDITIONAL PRACTICES

SPIRITUAL GROWTH AND MEDITATION PRACTICES

Additional integrative exercises, meditation practices and two case studies are provided on the following pages. You can do the exercises on your own or in a group setting. The content in this section can also be used to engage meaningful discussion with family, friends and group members.

Spiritual practice aligns the mental, emotional and physical bodies with the blissful consciousness of eternal truth.

Define the Following Terms

Use the information provided within the book to define the following terms:

1. Child consciousness:

2. Defense mechanism:

3. Fear:

4. Lower character traits:

5. Perception:

6. Presence:

7. Pride:

8. Self-image:

9. Self-will:

10. Spiritual Self:

Step by Step to Your Spiritual Self

Self-awareness and self-honesty opens the channel to your spiritual self. The following questions will help you gain inner clarity and access to your divine center.

1. Write down the emotional reactions you're having about the person or situation you are concerned about (i.e., jealousy, anger, conflict, confusion, frustration, etc.).

2. Describe your behaviors and how they affect the situation.

3. Are you aware of a self-image that you may be acting out? Are you aware of any pain that you may be resisting? If so, why?

4. What benefit do you receive by acting out your self-image or resisting your real feelings?

5. What is it that you really want from this person or situation?

6. Pray and ask your spiritual self to help you identify what you can change within to align with the truth.

Daily Meditation to Be Present

Your natural rhythm of peace and calm pulsates to the resonance of your spiritual self. Follow the steps below to help you align with your true self:

1. Set your intention to let go of any judgements, criticisms, attitudes or opinions that prevent you from experiencing your natural inner rhythm of peace and calm.

2. State an intention that will build a strong, positive force field. Example: "I choose to allow my inherent strengths to lead and guide my thoughts today" or "I commit to acknowledge and recognize my true self" Or "I will grant myself the necessary time to access the wisdom of my spiritual mind through daily meditation."

3. Allow your positive intentions to become a priority at the beginning of each day. (Negative force fields can initially be so strong that repetition and re-commitment throughout the day is necessary to diffuse the negative power.)

4. Support your intention throughout the day with positive actions and behavior.

5. Allow yourself to *feel* the emotions of these productive thoughts. (Positive magnetic force fields stimulate and enhance the electrical activity in the nervous system that increase the physical sensation of 'feeling good'.)

Sitting In Silence

Sitting in silence is a wonderful, meaningful way to connect with people. Whether it's in your home, workplace or school, create a designated area where you can sit in silence and just breathe together. Make sure the space is clean and uncluttered. Hang a sign that states the intention for the space. For example, 'Sitting Silently Together' or 'Being & Breathing Together'.

Let everyone know which room you plan to use. If it's a multi-purpose room, then set scheduled times so the people who are interested can join you. Although it's best to schedule a weekly routine time, you may have to set a few different times each week to accommodate varying schedules.

If it's at work, you can make an announcement through an e-mail blast or the employee newsletter. If it's at home, you can have a discussion with your family members about the benefits of a quiet space to calm the mind.

Practice may be necessary to achieve silence. Communicate to everyone that the space has been chosen specifically for silence and that this should be respected.

CASE STUDIES

African Crossbows

The following case study is from a session I had with a client whom I shall refer to as 'Lorraine'. Lorraine works out of her home. She suffers from intermittent physical pain in her upper body, mainly in her neck and shoulder. She says that she feels very isolated, lonely, and is having bouts of depression.

During the time of this call, Lorraine had been working on identifying the defense mechanisms she built as a child and how to access the truth from her higher self. The dialogue below is from part of that session. This session was conducted over the telephone.

L & K Dialogue:

K: …We also talked about your need for socializing and connection. You mentioned you would reach out to your neighbor during one of your long workdays for a break and to make connection. Were you able to make contact with her?

L: No. (sigh) I don't know how to get out of this rut. I feel like I need homework, even though you've already given me suggestions. (frustration) Assignments that I haven't done. I'm just going round in circles.

K: Well, it's important to acknowledge that you willingly do exercises during our sessions, while you have positive support and mirroring. My sense is that when you feel connected and engaged, you're motivated to express more of yourself. When you're alone, the cruelty of your lower self takes over.

L: Why?? How do I stop that?

K: The good news is the answer is inside of you. We can go deeper if you'd like to see what's blocking you from moving forward.

L: o.k. yes, let's do it.

I started as I always do and opened with a prayer:

K: God, please lead our session today and guide Lorraine as she opens up to the inner depths of her being. May Your voice within guide and illuminate the truth of Lorraine's inner most being.

K to Lorraine: I invite you, Lorraine, to surrender to the brilliance of your unconscious mind. As it presents itself to you, let me know what you're experiencing, whether it's a feeling, an image, a memory, or even unfamiliar thought-forms, sounds, could be colors. Relax and just allow yourself to receive what your inner self reveals to you.

After a few minutes of silence, Lorraine spoke.

L: I see several African men holding crossbows. They have shields.

K: Are you open to having a dialogue with them?

L: I'll try. (pause) I just asked them, 'Why are you here?' One of them responded, 'to protect you'.

K: From what?

L: I don't know. I have to ask. (pause) They're keeping me safe.

K: From what?

L: I don't know. From whatever's out there. They're saying, 'It's all she knows.'

K: Lorraine, does this make any sense to you?

L: Yes. This is how I live. I'm always so guarded.

K: Are you willing to observe yourself, in your mind's eye, standing across from the African men?

L: It's funny, as soon as you said that they shrunk into these miniature toy-like figures. I'm standing across from them and I'm much bigger than they are now.

K: How does it feel?

L: It feels good. I feel big and expanded and they're small. They're still there, but they're much tinier than me.

K: You know you can choose this expanded, good feeling outside of sessions too. You can choose *not* to go into 'crossbow' mode (defense mode).

L: But I'm so used to it. I get stuck in it because I don't even realize that I'm being defensive. (pause) … You know, as you were talking, something came to me [another state of consciousness breaking through] that I want to share with you. When I was younger, I remember getting gas and there were these three young guys in a car who were also getting gas. They were whistling and laughing, making crude gestures, blowing whistles, 'woo-hoo', you know, that kind of stuff. Sometimes it can be flattering, but really they're just being jerks (vacillation between states of consciousness).

K: Uh huh.

L: Well, I actually went up to their car and I said, "Can I help you with something?" And they were stunned. They all just froze and looked at me. They couldn't construct one sensible sentence. My point is those guys at the gas station are like the African men with the crossbows. As soon as I stood in front of them, they shrank.

K: As did your inner defense that says you should remain isolated and lonely to be protected from 'whatever's out there'.

L: Yes, yes. This is good. This makes sense.

Summary

You can usually identify the meaning of an image and what it's trying to convey by its 'tone', the form it represents, and your feelings toward it. For instance, the image of the crossbow represented Lorraine's *unconscious* misconception that it was safer not to speak up. She mistakenly believed that being silent offered her protection. As Lorraine confronted and dialogued with the image, she became aware of the misconception. Lorraine could then utilize her current life experiences at the gas station to re-educate this distortion with the truth.

Various Levels of Consciousness:
Child Consciousness
   a) Small and frozen in fear; perceives herself as a victim and assumes intimidation or attack.

Defense Mechanisms
   a) Resistance - Lorraine doesn't take action to feel better (i.e. chair yoga stretches or reach out to neighbors for connection)
   b) Manipulation – exaggerates/feigns danger to make Lorraine feel vulnerable and unsafe
   c) Lies to imply Lorraine is not enough as she is – 'I need more homework'.

Present Awareness
   a) Address the issue
   b) Set intention to willingly acknowledge, confront, and dialogue with herself
   c) Receive and respond to incoming information in present time
   d) Re-educate misconception with the truth

Spiritual Self
   a) Wisdom and clarity provide root cause of resistance
   b) Inner knowing provides strength and confidence
   c) Truth heals and courage is restored, even though there's more growth in store.

EXERCISE

1. Which spiritual laws would you focus on if you were in Lorraine's shoes?

2. How would the laws you chose help you to grow?

3. What would you have to change and let go of?

The Frozen Shoulder

The following case study was taken from a session I conducted over the telephone. For the purposes of confidentiality, I'll refer to my client as Julianne.

Julianne is working twelve to fourteen hour days, six days a week. Julianne wants to open a real estate business, but she doesn't have enough money. She says she can't rely on her husband because "he hasn't been making money for years". When I asked Julianne if she had discussed her career desires with her husband, she replied, "He doesn't listen. He sits in front of the television and nods, but he's not really there. I know he's just acquiescing by nodding yes."

Julianne has also been going to a physical therapist for a few weeks because of chronic arm and shoulder pain.

I led us in prayer and asked God to show us any resistances, misconceptions, attitudes, or beliefs that were contributing to Julianne's current state of physical and emotional pain.

After moments of silence, Julianne recalled an image of herself as a young child cleaning her mother's brass coffee table. I asked Julianne which arm in the image was doing the polishing. She replied that it was her right arm, the same one that she was currently having trouble with. When I asked what this image of the brass coffee table represented, Julianne explained that as a child, her mother would scream and yell incessantly. In a heightened state of anxiety, Julianne would clean excessively to get her mother to stop yelling. Julianne's pseudo-solution rarely worked, but it helped to busy and distract her from her mother's erratic outbursts.

Julianne also disclosed that her mother never allowed her husband, Julianne's father, to sit and eat with them at the dinner table. House rules by Julianne's mother dictated that she and her sister were not allowed to speak with their father at all. The few times that Julianne tried, her mother would interrupt with negative comments or shoot her silent, disapproving stares.

Julianne concluded at a young age it was easier just to ignore her father. We discussed Julianne's beliefs about receiving – from her family while growing up and from her husband currently. Julianne revealed, "I don't expect to get anything from anyone. I'll be independent and get whatever I want on my own."

When I asked Julianne about her relationship with God, she commented that she knows God by praying and asking for help, but never receives an answer. Julianne shared her conclusion (misconception), "God's probably too busy with other people."

We continued to discuss the importance of the brass table image and how it relates to her current situation. Julianne became very emotional stating, *"This is very painful because I see the connection. All my mother did was complain so I never dared to ask for anything. I wasn't allowed to speak to my father, so I couldn't ask him for support. And now I think the same thing about God. I don't expect a response. I don't expect to receive anything – from my husband or anyone else. Especially God. I just pray out of habit, but I now realize that I don't really believe I'll receive spiritual support. I'm going to do it all on my own, there's no one – or nothing spiritual – to turn to."*

Julianne and I spent time sorting through the distorted beliefs that she created in childhood. After a deep emotional release, Julianne centered herself. With her eyes closed, she prayed aloud asking God to be shown the truth.

After a few moments of silence, Julianne relayed a vision, *"Kathleen, I'm surrounded by several very large angelic-like figures. They're translucent, but I can make them out because they're outlined in brilliant pastel colors. I don't know how to describe this but it's like they're holding me – I'm immersed with them, but I'm still me. I'm one and yet different from them. I don't know how this sounds to you, but it feels so real. They want me to know, they're telling me 'I am supported. I am supported.'"*

These were the words that Julianne spoke as she received her 'transmission'. It was peaceful and in that peace we closed the session.

EXERCISE

1. Write down the spiritual laws that you would focus on if you were in Julianne's situation.

2. How would the laws help your spiritual growth? What would you have to change and let go of?

RELIGIOUS TENETS

Buddhism

The Four Noble Truths

- Suffering is a part of life.
- Suffering is caused by desire.
- There is an end to suffering.
- Follow the Noble Eightfold Path:

    1. Knowledge of the truth (Samma-Ditthi).
    2. The intention to resist evil (Samma-Sankappa).
    3. Say nothing to hurt others (Samma-Vaca).
    4. Respect life, mortality, and property (Samma-Kammanta).
    5. Hold a job that doesn't injure others (Samma-Ajiva).
    6. Strive to free one's mind (Samma-Vayama).
    7. Control one's feelings and thoughts (Samma-Sati).
    8. Practice proper forms of concentration (Samma-Samadhi).

Christianity

The New Testament

- This is my commandment, that ye love one another, as I have loved you. *(John 15:12)*
- It is written, Man shall not live by bread alone, but by every word that proceed out of the mouth of God. *(Matthew 4:4)*
- Except ye be converted, and become as little children, ye shall not enter into the kingdom of heaven. *(Matthew 18: 3-5)*
- Watch and pray, that ye enter not into temptation; the spirit indeed is willing, but the flesh is weak. *(Matthew, 26:41)*
- Ask, and it will be given to you; seek, and you will find; knock, and the door will be opened to you. *(Matthew 7:7-8)*
- Not that which goeth into the mouth defileth a man; but that which cometh out of the mouth, this defileth a man. *(Matthew 15:10-11)*
- Let your light so shine before men, that they may see your good works, and glorify your Father who is in heaven. *(Matthew 5:16)*

Hinduism

Niyama (Yoga or Scriptural rules)

- Purity (Shaucha): Excretion is purification and cleansing. Excretion or purification is of two types – one is external and one is internal.
    Purify body with water; purify mind with good behavior; purify soul by learning and devotion to purify intelligence with knowledge.
- Contentment (Santosh): One should fulfill one's objectives with the available resources. To be fully satisfied with whatever results are obtained, to not desire unobtainable objects, to not disregard achievements acquired with the grace of God, and to not aspire for what is not available is contentment.
- Penance (Tapas): Whatever pains, troubles, adversities come in the path of accomplishment of objectives, they should be accepted gracefully and we should march forward towards our goal continuously without deviating.
- Regular study of the Vedas (Swadhyay): Study the classics written by the sages and study knowing the self or, realizing the internal self.
- Deep devotion towards God (Ishwar Pranidhan): Devoting all our actions to God.

Judaism and Catholicism (Old Testament)
The Ten Commandments

- I am the Lord thy God, who brought thee out of the land of Egypt, out of the house of bondage.
- Thou shalt have no other gods before me.
- Thou shalt not take thy name of the Lord thy God in vain.
- Remember the Sabbath day to keep it holy.
- Honor thy father and thy mother.
- Thou shalt not murder.
- Thou shalt not commit adultery.
- Thou shalt not steal.
- Thou shalt not bear false witness against thy neighbor.
- Thou shalt not covet anything that belongs to thy neighbor.

Taoism

East Asian Philosophy

- Tao is the first-cause of the universe. It is a force that flows through all of life.
- The Tao surrounds everyone and therefore everyone must listen to find enlightenment.
- A believer's goal is to harmonize themselves with the Tao.
- The 'priesthood' views the many gods as manifestations of the one Tao, 'which could not be represented as an image or a particular thing.'
- Development of virtue is one's chief task: compassion, moderation, and humility.
- Taoists follow the art of 'wu wei' – allow nature to take its course.
- Plan in advance and consider carefully each action before taking it.
- People left to their own devices will show compassion without expecting a reward.
- Yin and Yang represent the balance of opposites in the universe. When equally present, all is calm.

BIBLIOGRAPHY

Alexander, Pagyn. *Dreamtime Magic*. Tennessee. Dragonhawk Publishing, 1987.

Brennan, Barbara Ann. *Hands of Light*. New York. Bantom Books, 1988.

Brennan, Barbara Ann. *Light Emerging*. New York. Bantom Books, 1993.

Bruyere, Rosalyn. *Wheels of Light*. New York. Touchstone. 1994.

Chopra, Deepak, M.D.. *How To Know God*. New York. Three Rivers Press, 2000.

Cousins, Norman. *The Healing Heart*. Canada. George J. McLeod Ltd, 1983.

Czuba, Cheryl, *UCONN PEP, People Empowering People*, Connecticut. UCONN Agriculture, Health and Natural Resources, 1996.

Dyer, Wayne, Ph.D. *Wisdom of the Ages*. New York. Harper Collins, 1999.

Forbes, Bo, Psy.D. *Yoga for Emotional Balance*. Massachusetts. Shambhala, 2011.

Garfield, Patricia, Ph.D. *Creative Dreaming*. New York. Fireside, 1995.

Gerber, Richard, M.D. *Vibrational Medicine*. Vermont, 2001.

Giovanni. *Types of Meditation – An Overview of 23 Meditation Techniques*. Stoll Foundation of Holistic Health

Juncos, Jorge, M.D., Ph.D, and Kathleen (Kiley) Fisher. *Spirituality and Modern Medicine: Science On A Wing and A Prayer?* Georgia. Emory Center for Complementary and Alternative Medicine, 2003.

Jung, Carl, M.D., Ph.D. *Dream Analysis.* New Jersey. Princeton University Press, 1984.

Jung, Carl, M.D., Ph.D. *Memories, Dreams, Reflections.* New York. Vintage Books, 1963.

Kelsey, Morton. *God, Dreams and Revelation.* Minnesota. Fortress Press, 1991.

LaBerge, Stephen, Ph.D. *Lucid Dreaming.* Colorado. Sounds True, 2009.

Lipton, Bruce. *Biology of Belief.* California. Hay House, 2008.

Martin, Steve. *Born Standing Up.* New York. Scribner, 2007.

Mauro, Colleen. *Spiritual Telepathy.* Illinois. Quest Books, 2015

McGonigal, K., Ph.D. *"Training for Mind-Body Resilience."* Fitness Journal. April, 2013.

Moore, Thomas. Care of the Soul. New York. Harper Perennial, 1994.

Mueser, K., Ph.D. *"The Effects of Yoga on Mood in Psychiatric Inpatients."* Psychosocial

Niebuhr, Reinhold, Reverend. *The Serenity Prayer*

Orloff, Judith, M.D. *Second Sight.* New York. Harmony, 2010

Pearson, Craig, Ph.D. *"The Kingdom of God Is Within You."* TM Blog. December 6, 2010.

Pierrokos, Eva. *Guide Lectures 1-258.* New York. The Pathwork Foundation, 1957-1979.

Pierrokos, Eva. *The Pathwork to Self-Transformation.* New York. Bantom Books, 1990.

Pierrokos, John, M.D. *Core Energetics.* New York. Core Evolution Publishing, 2005.

Pierrokos, Eva and Thesenga, Donovan. *Fear No Evil.* Virginia. Pathwork Press, 1997.

Ramdev, Swami. *Yoga: Its Philosophy & Practice.* Uttarakhand. Divya Prakashan, 2002.

Rocha, Tomas. *"The Dark Knight of the Soul."* The Atlantic. June 25, 2014.

Roger, Carl and Farson, Richard Evans. *Active Listening.* Martino Fine Books, September, 2015

Sanford, John. *Dreams. God's Forgotten Language.* California. HarperOne, 1989.

Savige, Craig. *"Electrical design in the human body."* Creation Magazine. December 1, 1999.

Schimoff, Marci. *Happy for No Reason.* New York. Atria Books, 2009.

Shealy, Norman, M.D., Ph.D. *Sacred Healing*. United Kingdom. Element Books, 2001.

Spolin, Viola. *Improvisation for the Theater*, Northwestern University Press, 1999.

Targ, Russel. *Miracles of the Mind*. California. New World Library, 1998.

Thesenga, Susan. *The Undefended Self*. Virginia. Pathwork Press, 2001.

Thurston, Mark. *How To Interpret Your Dreams*. Virginia, A.R.E. Press, 1978.

Van Der Castle, Robert, Ph.D. *Our Dreaming Mind*. New York. Ballantine Books, 1995.

Weil, Andrew, M.D. *Spontaneous Healing*. New York. Ballantine Books, 2000.

Young, Sarah. *Jesus Calling*. Kansas, Hallmark Gift Books, 2004.

Zukav, Gary. *Seat of the Soul*. New York. Simon and Schuster, 2014.

ON-LINE RESOURCES

bible.com

biblegateway.com

buddhanet.net

clinicaltrials.gov

ergo.human.cornell.edu

ezinearticles.com

jewishvirtuallibrary.org

medlineplus.gov

ncbi.nlm.nih.gov

nccam.nih.gov

orthoinfo.org

osha.gov

putumayo.com

quantumtechniques.com

religioustolerance.org

the torah.com

tm.org

ABOUT THE AUTHOR

Kathleen is a Pathwork Teacher and offers Pathwork classes, workshops, and tutorials. Kathleen has created several Wellness and Spirituality programs for hospitals, correctional institutions, and behavioral health agencies. In addition to 'The Spiritual Mind', Kathleen has also authored 'Destress With Mind, Body, and Breath' and 'Wellness Lessons for Social Emotional Learning'.

Kathleen lives in New England with her husband Daniel and their dog, Jean-Pierre.

Contact Information:
Wellness Insights, LLC
Mind Body Spirit for Health
www.kathleenkileyfisher.com
kathleenkileyfisher@gmail.com

www.ingramcontent.com/pod-product-compliance
Lightning Source LLC
Chambersburg PA
CBHW080338170426
43194CB00014B/2615